GIZZI'S HEALTHY APPETITE

FOOD TO NOURISH THE BODY AND FEED THE SOUL

GIZZI'S HEALTHY APPETITE

FOOD TO NOURISH THE BODY AND FEED THE SOUL

GIZZI ERSKINE

INTERLINK BOOKS, AN IMPRINT OF INTERLINK PUBLISHING GROUP, INC.
www.interlinkbooks.com

CONTENTS

INTRODUCTION

There's no denying that I have a healthy appetite. I *love* food, I *love* eating, and I *love* cooking. There's nothing I don't like to eat, except perhaps snow peas (pointless and flabby) and durian (poo fruit). I am a chef for two reasons: partly because I have a huge ego and I love feeding people and receiving their praise, but mainly because food makes people happy and has a way of soothing us from the inside out. Food doesn't just feed my body, it also feeds my soul.

I've written about healthy eating over the years, but recently I've seen an influx of books encouraging us to "eat clean," make better choices, become vegan for our health, or undertake extreme diets—and no one knows what the best advice actually is.

The more I see of people's food concerns on Twitter and Instagram, the more I see the love pouring out of food. It's as though people are so concerned about what they are putting into their bodies that food has lost its soul. Food should first and foremost be delicious. If we stick to some simple rules like eating a variety of different-colored fruits and vegetables daily, eating smaller portions of better carbs, high-quality proteins, and some good fats, then we will be getting all the nutrition we need for optimum health.

Back when I made *Cook Yourself Thin*, we were using vegetables in place of carbohydrates, choosing non-starchy carbs for mashing, and putting vegetables in cakes to reduce the sugar and fat content. Now, there are some brilliant new techniques to make things like vegan, gluten-free, and sugar-free cakes; cauliflower rice; and spiralized vegetable noodles, all of which can be a revelation when used in the right way with the right ingredients.

Cooking for a healthy appetite often seems to be geared more towards the healthy and less towards an appetite for food. However, I want to show you how to use those "healthy" ingredients in a more delicious way. I also want to instill the message that being healthy is as much about moderation as it is about nutrition. I've always lived by the 80/20 rule: if you eat healthily 80 percent of the time then you're allowed a little bit of something that may be considered "naughty" the rest of the time.

The chapters of this book are divided into textures and flavors. For me, those textures and flavors often reflect my mood. For example, if I crave something braised or oozy it may mean that I'm after something rib-sticking and comforting, but if I want crunch or crispness then I probably feel the need for something clean and fresh. Sometimes I want fiery food, so we have a chapter for spice, and other times I just need something sweet, and there's a chapter for that too.

So, here I am. I want to start a new food revolution: one where people have a better understanding of nutrition but don't forget that eating should be enjoyable.

MY ETHOS

Every week when I open up a newspaper or magazine, there's a new bit of health information that puts a wrench in the works of what I had previously thought was the right way to be healthy. So here is my ethos, and a bit about how I feel about food trends and what we can learn from them.

Firstly, I believe that having a better understanding of nutrition is not just about making your body healthier, it can also make you a better cook. The more I learn about different ingredients or come across new cooking techniques, vegetables, or cuts of meat, the more inspired I tend to be. I want this book to teach you that it's good to love food in all its guises and that sometimes your body needs to be fed what it's craving. Ultimately, I want the people reading this book to try new things and push themselves into new areas of food, be it going to your local Asian supermarket or having a go at cooking with a new ingredient or gadget. I hope to inspire people to cook fresh food using good ingredients.

THE 80/20 RULE

I follow the 80/20 rule. I'm good most of the time but absolutely allow myself to eat what I want the rest of the time, just so long as the food's been made with fresh ingredients. That said, I'm partial to a bit of processed cheese in my hamburger and I am going to eat it every so often—so sue me! The 80/20 rule can be applied daily, but I think it works best when you eat healthily during the week and have a blow-out one day of the weekend and perhaps the odd dinner out.

There's also another way you can apply the 80/20 rule: have 20 percent less food on your plate, eat 20 percent fewer carbohydrates, and eat 20 percent more vegetables. This will allow you to eat pretty much what you want, but you will be consuming 300-400 fewer calories a day. It's a simple but good rule to stick to.

CARBS

The glycaemic index (GI) scale shows how quickly blood sugar levels are raised after eating particular foods. Things like protein and green veggies barely register on the scale, making them very low GI, and whole grains are also low GI because your body has to fight to digest them. Whereas, sugars, many fruits, and processed white carbohydrates will make your blood sugar levels shoot up, releasing insulin into the blood and allowing the body to lay down fat. Because of this, I try to eat foods that are low GI whenever I can.

I'm pro-carbs but I do think it's important not to eat too many of them. We should be averaging (depending on gender and height) about 60-100g (in weight) of carbohydrates per meal, which, shockingly, is just a small bowl of pasta, an open sandwich, or a handful of rice. Start tracking your carbs and you'll soon see that you eat more than you should. My theory is that it's better to eat some carbs than none.

SUGAR

It's a sad fact that if we eat a balanced diet of carbohydrates, dairy, protein, fruit, and vegetables then we are already consuming the right amount of sugar for our bodies—and those who eat lots of carbs and fruit may be consuming too much sugar. This means that the addition of refined sugar into our diet can wreak havoc with our blood sugar levels. Just so long as we don't go crazy, a small amount of cake, chocolate, or sweets isn't going to affect us *that* badly, but it's definitely something we should be aware of.

When you process sugar you remove the small amount of fiber that allows your body to absorb the sugar straight into the bloodstream. While there are lots of great-tasting unrefined sugars available, not many of them work in the same way that refined cane sugar does in cooking, which can be a royal pain in the ass. If you simply want to add some sweetness to something, that's fine, but if you're trying to make a meringue, cake, or brownie, things can go horribly wrong. Trust me, I've done an absurd amount of tests trying to make this work so you don't have to. Wherever possible, I have used unrefined (or less refined) sweeteners in my recipes (like maple syrup, muscovado, or palm sugar). You can, if you like, use other sugars in any recipes that aren't for meringues, cakes, or brownies. My favorite alternatives are coconut palm nectar, coconut sugar, agave nectar, and rapadura sugar. You may need to experiment with them, since they all have varying degrees of sweetness.

FAT

Fat is back! We've known for ages that we should be eating good vegetable oils, such as olive, canola, avocado, and fish oils because they contain a mixture of omega fatty acids and vitamin E. Now, we also have coconut oil, which, despite being a saturated fat, is brilliant for metabolizing fat. And the best news of all is that butter is okay again and ghee is even better! In fact, it now seems that butter is not just okay, it's as good for you as any other fat.

So what went wrong? In the late 1950s a study was released that showed countries that ate more fat had higher rates of heart disease, so government guidelines told people to eat less saturated fat (including butter). Since then more research has been done to show that it isn't as simple as that and you need both fat and cholesterol in your diet. Fat does not make you fat. Butter and ghee contain good fats and vitamins that lower your risk of a heart attack compared to margarine. Butter makes veggies taste awesome due to fat-soluble vitamins in the veggies, and ghee is better than vegetable oil for cooking, since it is more stable at high temperatures.

My advice is to use a mixture of all of these different oils, eat 2-3 portions of oily fish a week, as well as eating nuts, seeds, and avocados. Just because all of these things have the potential to make you fat doesn't mean you don't need them in your diet in order to make your body work.

MEAT

If there is one thing that you take away from this book, let it be this: eat better protein and eat less of it. It is easy to overeat everything (carbs, fat, sugar, booze, and meat) and this has an effect on our bodies. However, eating too much meat also has an effect on the environment. The way we're going, it is looking increasingly likely that we will not be able to continue to consume meat the way we do today. We should be eating less meat, and the meat we eat should be better quality.

I always recommend buying meat from a butcher and using small producers who rear animals ethically and butcher in a more skilled way. This is my only mega-snobbery and it's also about animal welfare and the environment. I'm not pushing organic, I just want you to buy the best meat you can afford.

VEGETABLES

Vegetables (and fruit) are full of micronutrients. In most cases, we get more nutrients into our system if food is eaten raw, so eat tons of raw veggies, fruits, and salads. Green juices are a great way to absorb these nutrients into the body quickly, but I think these juices should be a supplement not a substitute for food. Most green vegetables are alkalizing and help us maintain a better pH in our bodies, which is why everyone is going greens crazy—keep up this trend. "An avocado a day keeps the wrinkles at bay" is my new theory and "eat more veggies" is my motto. So play around with vegetables: roast them, mash them, spiralize them, rice them, juice them, and make salads—just make sure over 50 percent of your daily food intake is made up of them.

DAIRY

If you really and truly have a dairy intolerance, avoid soy milk because a lot of it is made from GM crops, it's highly processed, and it's just not very tasty. Go for cold-pressed almond milks, since they are without doubt the tastiest, though I have also tasted some delicious hazelnut and macadamia nut milks.

STOCK

I've always used fresh stock in my food and have preached about it from the hilltops. Why on earth would you cook fresh food and then ram a sodium-filled bouillon cube into it? It's the biggest oxymoron in cooking. Fresh is always best when it comes to stock: for flavor, for clarity, and also for its gelatinous and health-giving properties. Marrow bones are super for you, and bone broth or stock is full of calcium and collagen and is also hydrating and anti-inflammatory. If you want a glossy, restaurant-quality gravy or sauce, fresh stock will reduce to a perfectly flavored, lip-smacking consistency.

THE MODERN KITCHEN

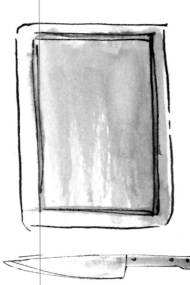

This new way of cooking may require some new equipment. Here's my list of kitchen must-haves:

A good knife and chopping board
These two things can be expensive, despite them being at the heart of almost every dish. Yes, you can go and grab yourself a knife and board from the supermarket but that will hold you back a bit as a cook. The way I see it, a good knife is for life, whereas the cheaper ones need replacing every 2–3 years. I buy Kin knives for value or go to the Japanese Knife Company if I want to splurge. The same ethos is true for a board. A wooden chopping board will last forever (just look at butchers' blocks) but plastic or glass will need replacing—and don't get me started on how they ruin your knives.

Nonstick pans
Cooking with a nonstick pan means that you need less oil, so they are essential if you're trying to cook with less fat. Go for a really heavy-based one—I love the toughened nonstick pans from Le Creuset.

A grill pan
An essential pan for modern cooking, and I use mine at least three times a week. The grill lines add caramelization and barbecue flavor to meat, fish, vegetables, or bread. I like a grill pan with wider ridges, since the thinner ones can make your food taste a little too barbecued. Always buy a really heavy cast-iron grill pan—the lighter ones don't add the flavor you need and fall to pieces.

A really good Dutch oven
I couldn't live without my cast-iron Dutch ovens. They are more important to me than almost any other kitchen equipment. The last couple of years has seen the rise of the slow cooker, but no slow cooker can do what a lidded, cast-iron Dutch oven can do, be it on the stovetop or in a low oven. For slow cooking, a really good Dutch oven is unbeatable.

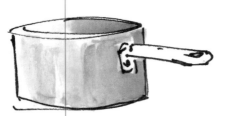

Tons of mixing bowls

Ideally, you should have a mixture of glass and metal bowls in a variety of sizes to meet every kitchen eventuality.

Electric weighing scales

Scales are essential to make sure you're not eating too much. Over-consuming is such a common problem that it's worth getting into the boring habit of weighing out your food, especially carbohydrates. I prefer electric scales as they are more precise.

A spiralizer

A spiralizer is a great way to cut back on carbs and eat more fresh vegetables and it's really worth the money. If you can't afford one, a hand-held vegetable ribboner will do the same thing and you'll build muscles in the process.

A powerful blender

A pretty kitchen blender just won't do in my eyes. It's more important to consider the power of a blender: the higher the power, the finer the blend. Vitamix blenders are the best, blending smoothies, soups, and pastes to oblivion, but are very expensive so buy the best you can afford.

A food processor

I use a food processor almost every day, for everything from making pastes to cauliflower rice.

A stand mixer

This is a gadget that's on most people's kitchen wish lists. You need a stand mixer to whisk, beat, or knead food so it's a baking gadget. I lived with my KitchenAid for years but got an Electrolux Grand Cuisine stand mixer this year and it's been a game-changer. If a mixer is too pricey, use an electric hand mixer for whisking and beating.

SLURP

SMOOTHIES, SOUPS & NOODLES

BANANA, DATE, ALMOND MILK & BEE POLLEN SMOOTHIE

My friend Elly, who owns the Pear Café in Bristol, is a genius when it comes to healthy cooking. She has been doing the 5:2 diet for a couple of years and has not only lost over 30 pounds, but also created some of the most brilliant recipes. Her knowledge of ingredients is second to none. When we were hanging out in Spain, she introduced me to bee pollen because I get terrible allergies and have the worst allergic reaction to insect bites—and the bee pollen genuinely helped. That is what bee pollen is best known for but it also does a multitude of other things: it boosts energy, smoothes the skin, is an anti-inflammatory for the respiratory system, has enzymes to aid digestion, and helps the cardiovascular system. It really is a superfood. I drink one of these smoothies in the morning and it kicks me in the butt. I feel better for doing so and I swear my allergies have gone away.

··

As with any smoothie recipe, it's all about the blender. I like to use the most powerful blender available (see page 13).

Place the ingredients into a blender in the order stated and blitz for 1 minute if you have a powerful blender or 1 minute 20 seconds if your blender is the classic type. Pour into glasses and serve.

2 bananas (the ripest you can find, since they are sweetest), peeled, cut into chunks, and frozen
6 soft pitted dates (the best quality you can afford)
1 tablespoon bee pollen
2 cups (500ml) really good pressed almond milk

SUPER GREEN SMOOTHIE

Everybody's doing it, so you might as well do it too. This is the power juice of all power juices and it will give you the biggest spring in your step you could ever want. Any good blender will do. The apples and pears will add tons of sweetness and be the liquid in the smoothie; the kale is alkaline, which will balance your pH levels; the avocado has vitamin E and good oils that help burn fat and will make you look radiant; and the herbs provide an abundance of antioxidants. Drink this for breakfast with a handful of almonds to give yourself a protein boost. You will be bouncing off the walls before you know it!

Juice the apples and pears.

Next, place the rest of the ingredients in a blender in the order they are listed, along with the juices. Blend for 1 minute, or until totally smooth: the kale can take a while to blend. Once it is smooth, divide between 2 tall glasses and serve with a straw.

4 Granny Smith apples
5 pears
juice of 1 lemon
1 kiwi, peeled and frozen in
   chunks
1 avocado, peeled, pitted, and
   chopped
1 tablespoon pea or hemp
   protein (optional)
a good handful of green kale,
   trimmed of its stems and
   chopped
a good handful of mint
a good handful of parsley

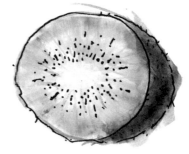

CHILLED CUCUMBER, AVOCADO & BUTTERMILK SOUP

Chilled soups are one of the greatest things about summer. This is a really simple one made with buttermilk, which has a slight tang, alongside cucumber, avocado, dill, and mint. The cucumber is the base flavor; the avocado is mainly there for texture, making the soup silky; and the dill and mint just add freshness. Make it in the morning and allow to homogenize for a few hours in the fridge, then eat for a late-summer lunch when the soup's extra cold, adding a few ice cubes if you like.

Coarsely chop 5 of the cucumber halves and transfer to a large bowl. Add the buttermilk, lemon juice, scallions, dill, mint, garlic, and salt and pepper. Stir to combine, cover with plastic wrap, and leave to stand at room temperature for 1 hour to blend the flavors. Dice the remaining cucumber half and set aside until ready to serve.

In a powerful blender, purée the cucumber mixture, together with the avocado, until smooth. With the machine running, slowly add the stock and purée until it is fully incorporated; this will take about 30 seconds. Transfer to a jug, cover with plastic wrap, and refrigerate for about 2 hours, or until chilled.

Pour the soup into bowls, then top with the chopped cucumber and drizzle with the oil and a little extra buttermilk. Garnish with the extra mint and dill and serve immediately.

3 medium cucumbers, halved
  lengthways and deseeded
1 cup (250ml) buttermilk, plus
  extra to serve
2 tablespoons lemon juice
2 scallions (green and white
  parts), chopped
3 tablespoons chopped dill,
  plus extra to garnish
a few mint leaves, plus extra
  tiny mint leaves to garnish
1 small garlic clove, chopped
sea salt flakes and white pepper
1 large ripe but firm avocado,
  peeled and pitted
1¾ cups (420ml) fresh White
  Chicken or Veggie Stock
  (see pages 212–13), chilled
2 tablespoons really good,
  fruity extra virgin olive oil

PREPARATION TIME
25 minutes, plus chilling

COOKING TIME
30 minutes

CHLODNIK
(CHILLED POLISH BEET SOUP WITH DILL PICKLES, EGGS & SHRIMP)

As far as chilled soups go, chlodnik has to be one of the unsung heroes. It's basically borscht that is enriched with buttermilk and sour cream and topped with an array of jazzy things like peeled shrimp, boiled eggs, pickles, and mounds of dill. With her Polish heritage, my mother always waxed lyrical about buying bottles of borscht as a teen and pimping it up with way too much sour cream, making it look a little like Pepto-Bismol! She has a point, but this soup tastes anything but. Making this soup is a really great way to use up a glut of beets in the winter—just freeze and turn it into a terrific dish in the summer.

•••

Heat the oil in a large saucepan. Add the onion and cook over low heat for about 10 minutes, or until translucent and softened enough that you can squish through the onion with your fingertips. Add the beets and cucumber and cook for 10 minutes, or until the beets start to break down. Pour in the stock and cook at an aggressive simmer for a further 10 minutes, or until the beets are really soft.

Remove from the heat and stir in the buttermilk and sour cream. Using either a blender or immersion blender, blitz the soup for about a minute, or until it's completely smooth: it should be the thickness of light cream. You can strain the soup at this point if you like it extra smooth (I do!). Season with salt and pepper and the pickle brine and leave to cool, then throw it in the fridge to chill for at least 5 hours. I always like to put the soup in the freezer for 30 minutes before serving to get it really chilled.

Ladle the soup into bowls and top each bowl of soup with 3 of the egg quarters. Add some pickles, shrimp, and dill before serving with extra buttermilk drizzled with olive oil.

1 tablespoon olive oil, plus extra to serve
1 onion, finely chopped
4 beets, peeled and grated
1 Lebanese or Persian cucumber or ½ regular cucumber, peeled and grated
2½ cups (600ml) fresh White Chicken or Veggie Stock (see pages 212–13)
2 cups (500ml) buttermilk, plus extra to serve
2 cups (500ml) sour cream
sea salt flakes and freshly ground black pepper
3 tablespoons dill pickle brine

To serve

5 free-range eggs, hard-boiled and cut into quarters
2 dill pickles, chopped
½lb (200g) cooked, peeled small shrimp (I prefer Atlantic shell-on baby shrimp, peeled)
a small bunch of dill, roughly chopped

SERVES 4
....

PREPARATION TIME
20 minutes

COOKING TIME
50 minutes

MULLIGATAWNY SOUP WITH POACHED EGGS & CRISPY SHALLOTS

Mulligatawny is an Anglo-Indian soup that is curried and thickened with lentils or rice—sometimes with meat, sometimes without. My version is a chicken-based soup that's spiced and thickened with lentils, but I've made more of a meal out of it with a soft-poached egg perched on the top and some crispy shallots. I make a batch of this soup for dinner on a Sunday night and serve it this way, then eat it with chopped-up boiled eggs the next day when I'm at work. Everyone is jealous of me when I have this lunch—it's epic.

....

3 tablespoons ghee or vegetable oil
6 free-range chicken thighs, skin on, bone in
sea salt flakes and freshly ground black pepper
1 large onion, finely chopped
6 garlic cloves, finely chopped
½ green chili
1in (3cm) piece of fresh ginger root, peeled and grated
1½ tablespoons ground cumin
1 tablespoon ground coriander
1 teaspoon ground turmeric
½ teaspoon cumin seeds
½ teaspoon coriander seeds
½ teaspoon black mustard seeds
2 dried chilies
1 cup (200g) red lentils
8½ cups (2 liters) fresh White Chicken or Veggie Stock (see pages 212–13)
scant 1 cup (200ml) coconut milk
juice of ¼ lemon
a small bunch of fresh cilantro, roughly chopped

For the garnish

4 free-range eggs, poached (I use pasture-raised eggs, since they have orange yolks)
plain yogurt
Crispy Shallots (see page 79)

Heat 2 tablespoons of the ghee or vegetable oil in a deep saucepan over medium-high heat. Season the chicken pieces with salt and pepper and then fry them in batches until browned all over. Remove the chicken with a slotted spoon and set aside.

Meanwhile, place the onion, garlic, chili, ginger, and ground spices in a food processor and process to make a curry paste.

Once all the chicken is browned, add the remaining ghee or vegetable oil to the pan and fry the whole spices and chilies for 1 minute, or until they start to pop. Add the curry paste and cook slowly for 5 minutes or until the paste is less "wet" and has started to tinge golden. Add the lentils, stock, and coconut milk and return the chicken to the pan. Cook for 45 minutes, or until the chicken is cooked through and easily peeled from the bone and the lentils are completely soft.

Using tongs, remove the chicken from the pan and set aside. When it is cool enough to handle, remove the skin and use 2 forks to shred the meat off the bone (one fork to hold the chicken steady and the other to tear the meat apart).

In the meantime, keep cooking the soup until the liquid has reduced by about ½in (1cm) and the stock has become rich and full of flavor, then season with plenty of salt and pepper. Return the shredded chicken to the pan. Remove from the heat, add the lemon juice and half the cilantro, and check the seasoning. Serve immediately, each bowl of soup topped with a poached egg, a swirl of yogurt, some crispy shallots, and more cilantro.

CHICKEN PHO WITH DAIKON NOODLES

After I'd caught the spiralizing bug, it was then a matter of seeing how it could be utilized. Spiralizing doesn't fit into every type of recipe, and it's wrong to just use it as a pasta or noodle substitute. The way to get the best out of spiralizing is to make the vegetable work for the dish. This pho is a great example of that— the daikon noodles complement the flavor of the classic Vietnamese broth. What you have here is a highly delicious, nutritious, health-giving, no-carb soup that can be eaten as a low-calorie lunch, or even as a snack through the day. What I tend to do is make the broth and save it in jars and put the spiralized daikon and all the accompaniments in a separate lunch bowl. This way when you get to work you can heat up the broth until it's piping hot and then serve it with all the bits. Less of a game changer and more of a life changer.

1 whole medium free-range chicken
1¾ cups (400ml) fresh White Chicken Stock (see page 212)
2 onions, roughly sliced
1in (3cm) piece of fresh ginger root, peeled and sliced
1 garlic bulb, cut in half horizontally
6 black peppercorns
1 star anise
1 cinnamon stick
1 lemongrass stalk, bashed
1 teaspoon salt
2 tablespoons fish sauce, and maybe some extra for a final season
2 teaspoons palm sugar
2 daikon radishes, about 1lb (400g)

To serve

2 Thai red chilies, finely sliced
2-3 scallions (green part only), finely sliced,
1 onion, very finely sliced into rings
a small handful of cilantro
a few sprigs of Thai basil
a handful of bean sprouts
1 lime, cut into 8 wedges

You will also need a spiralizer (see page 13)

Put the chicken in a large Dutch oven, together with the stock, onions, ginger, garlic, peppercorns, star anise, cinnamon stick, lemongrass, salt, fish sauce, and palm sugar, then top up with water until the chicken is covered. Bring to a boil, then reduce the heat and simmer for 1½ hours with the lid on, then take the chicken out and set aside to cool.

Strain the cooking vegetables out of the liquid, and then pour the broth into a saucepan and reduce down for about 30 minutes until you have a rich, flavorsome chicken broth. You may need to season it with more fish sauce at this stage.

While the broth is reducing and when the chicken is cool enough to handle, shred the chicken and spiralize the daikon and set aside.

Place a quarter of the spiralized daikon into each soup bowl and top with the shredded chicken, chilies, scallions, sliced onion, cilantro, Thai basil, and bean sprouts. Once you are happy with the flavor of the chicken broth, pour about 1 cup (250ml) into each bowl and leave for few minutes before serving with lime wedges.

SERVES 2
....

PREPARATION TIME
20 minutes

COOKING TIME
40–50 minutes

SAMGYETANG
(GINSENG BABY CHICKEN SOUP)

½ cup (75g) Korean or Japanese short grain rice

2 tablespoons (25g) sprouted Korean mixed rice (if you can't find this just increase the amount of short grain rice to ½ cup/100g)

2 small, free-range baby chickens (squab chicken or poussin)

3 small ginseng roots

5 ginkgo beans (optional)

a few jujubes (Korean or Chinese dates)

a few slices of fresh ginger root, peeled

8 garlic cloves

2 cups (500ml) White Chicken Stock (see page 212; the stock must be cold)

6 scallions, plus 2 very thinly sliced scallions (green parts only)

Gizzi's Kimchi (see page 217), to serve

For the dipping salt

1 teaspoon salt

¼ teaspoon white pepper

¼ teaspoon black pepper

pinch of sugar

Samgyetang is one of the purest dishes I've eaten and it's also one of the most health-giving dishes in Korean cooking, since its main ingredient is ginseng. This soup is reminiscent of what I consider to be the best kind of cold-busting foods, such as Jewish chicken noodle soup or Vietnamese Pho. Ginseng is expensive and can be hard to come by, though if you go to Chinatown or visit a Chinese doctor you will find it in abundance. If you find it hard to obtain ginseng, you can use a pinch of ginseng tea in the same way. To make this soup, you stuff baby chickens with Korean rice and some aromatics and then poach them in a stock with more of the same aromatics. The rice cooks inside the chicken and the dish is ready when the chicken is falling off the bone. Serve the soup with a dipping salt and kimchi.

Soak both types of rice in a bowl of water for 1 hour.

Strain the rice and stuff each chicken with half of the rice, a ginseng root, a ginkgo bean, a jujube, a slice of ginger, and 2 garlic cloves.

Put the stuffed chickens into a large cast-iron Dutch oven. Pour in the stock and 2 cups (500ml) water, and then add the remaining aromatics and the whole scallions to the pot. Simmer over medium heat for 40–50 minutes, or until cooked through. The chickens don't have to be completely immersed in liquid, since you are braising them and you want the soup to reduce a little so that it becomes richly flavored by the end of the cooking time. When cooked properly, the chicken can be easily pulled apart by chopsticks.

Meanwhile, make the dipping salt by mixing together all the ingredients in a small serving bowl or dipping bowl. Add half the dipping salt to the soup and stir. Transfer a chicken to each serving bowl, ladle over the soup, and finish by sprinkling on the sliced scallions. I like to dip the chicken into the dipping salt and serve the Kimchi in a small bowl alongside the soup.

MUL NAENGMYEON
(COLD KOREAN NOODLE SALAD)

I first had this salad at a proper Korean barbecue restaurant in Korea on the island of Jeju. The most interesting thing about the dish was the salad that they served alongside. It was an ice-cold buckwheat noodle salad covered in a sticky, acidic, but searingly spicy dressing accompanied by cucumber and boiled eggs. I've researched this recipe to death and although I tried it with pork, it is sometimes served with rare beef. The coolest thing about this dish is that it's served with ice-cold beef stock that chills the salad right down. It's a weird thing for a westerner but if you've ever had a bullshot (beef stock, vodka, Worcestershire sauce, and Tabasco sauce) you will understand why this is a winner!

....

1in (2cm) thick piece of sirloin
  steak, about 1lb (400g)
sea salt flakes and freshly
  ground black pepper
1 tablespoon cooking oil
7oz (200g) buckwheat soba
  noodles
2 tablespoons sugar
scant ½ cup (100ml) rice wine
  vinegar
5 tablespoons (100g) gochujang
  (Korean chili paste)
2 tablespoons sesame oil
2 cups (500ml) fresh Beef Stock
  (see page 213), chilled
½ Korean pear or a really firm
  regular pear, julienned
¼ cucumber, julienned
¼ daikon radish, julienned
2 scallions, very finely sliced
  into rings
2 free-range eggs, hard boiled
  for 8 minutes, chilled and
  peeled
toasted sesame seeds, to
  sprinkle (I like a mixture
  of white and black)

Season the steak with salt and pepper. Heat a large frying pan until lightly smoking. Add the oil and then sear the steak for 1 minute on each side. You want the steak to be somewhere between blue and medium-rare but with some serious char on the outside. Remove from the pan and leave to rest while you get on with making the rest of the salad.

Bring a pan of water to a boil and season with plenty of salt. Add the noodles and cook for 1 minute less than the package instructions. This will make sure the noodles are nice and al dente. Drain and refresh under cold running water, then throw into a bowl of iced water to chill them quickly. They need to be really cold.

Heat the sugar and vinegar in a small saucepan until the sugar dissolves and it becomes a light syrup. Whisk in the gochujang, then the sesame oil, and remove from the heat. You now have your dressing.

Do not heat the stock. The point of this recipe is that the stock is served chilled. Pour the stock into 4 bowls. Add the noodles in a neat swirl—Korean food is all about presentation—and cover with 2½ tablespoons of the dressing.

Thinly slice the beef, place it to the side of the noodles, and pour over the pan juices. Lay the cucumber, radish, and scallion slices to the side of the beef, then place half an egg next to the salad. Finish by topping with more dressing, if needed, and a good sprinkling of sesame seeds.

SERVES 4
....

PREPARATION TIME
25 minutes

COOKING TIME
15 minutes

TOM YUM GOONG
(HOT & SOUR FISH STEW)

1 tablespoon vegetable oil

1 lemongrass stick, very thinly
    sliced

4–5 thin slices of fresh ginger
    root

3–4 garlic cloves, thinly
    sliced

¾lb (350g) baby plum tomatoes,
    halved

1¾ cups (400ml) fresh White
    Chicken Stock (see page 212)

2 tablespoons lime juice

2–3 tablespoons fish sauce

5–7 makrut lime leaves
    (sometimes called kaffir lime
    leaves), thinly sliced

12 raw jumbo shrimp, peeled,
    deveined, and cut quite
    deeply down the back

1 sea bream, filleted and each
    fillet cut into 4, lengthways

1 squid, gutted, slashed, and
    cut into bite-sized pieces

sea salt flakes

a good handful of Thai holy
    basil

Crispy Shallots (see page 79),
    to garnish

cilantro leaves, to garnish

banh cuon rice wrappers, or
    rice noodles, or rice, to
    serve

For the paste

3 shallots

3 lemongrass sticks, bashed and
    root removed

1½in (4cm) piece of galangal
    (or fresh ginger root)

5 makrut lime leaves (sometimes
    called kaffir lime leaves),
    thinly sliced

6 Thai bird's eye chilies

1 teaspoon Thai roasted chili
    paste or hot red chili powder

½ teaspoon dried shrimp paste

1 teaspoon palm or brown sugar

5 cilantro roots

I really love tom yum goong, the hot and sour shrimp soup from Thailand. There's also a similar dish from Cambodia called solmar machoor, which is a soupy fish stew that is as fiery as it is sour—this is my take on them both. All the legwork for this stew is in the paste and in cooking down the tomatoes, so it's really important that you take your time and do this slowly to encourage the natural sweetness you want from the dish. I've served the stew with something completely odd—Vietnamese banh cuon rice wrappers, which I've used like big, fat, wide noodles. If you can't find them, any Vietnamese rice noodle will do or you can even use rice, which is wicked to soak up the stew.

....

To make the paste, pound together all the ingredients to form a smoothish paste. I prefer to do this using a mortar and pestle, but this can be time-consuming so pulse the ingredients in a food processor or blender if you're in a rush.

Heat the oil in a large saucepan. Fry the lemongrass, ginger, and garlic for 2 minutes. This is a little unconventional but it will give the stew a deeper, more caramelized flavor. Add 3 tablespoons of the prepared paste and fry for 1 minute, then add the tomatoes and cook for 3 minutes, or until they start to melt. Pour in the stock, lime juice, fish sauce, and lime leaves and cook for 5 minutes. Add the shrimp, fish, and squid, season with salt, and cook for 3–4 minutes, or until the seafood is just cooked and the shrimp are pink. Stir through the holy basil and garnish with Crispy Shallots and cilantro leaves. Serve the stew with flat rice wrappers, rice noodles, or rice.

PIMPED-UP PAD THAI

½ tablespoon vegetable oil

1¾oz (50g) strip of firm tofu (4in/10cm long, ½in/1cm wide, and about ¼in/8mm thick)

½ banana shallot, thinly sliced

5 raw jumbo shrimp, peeled and deeply deveined (I leave the tails on)

1 free-range egg

3½oz (100g) pad Thai noodles, soaked for 20 minutes, then drained

3 tablespoons fresh White Chicken Stock (see page 212)

2 teaspoons (5g) finely chopped salted radish (you can't substitute this, so just leave out if you can't find it)

1¾oz (50g) bean sprouts

5 long garlic chives, each cut into 6 pieces

For the pad Thai sauce

1 tablespoon Sriracha chili sauce

1 tablespoon palm or light muscovado sugar

3 tablespoons tamarind paste (made from rehydrating tamarind)

1 tablespoon oyster sauce

1 tablespoon fish sauce

½ teaspoon Maggi liquid seasoning (optional)

To serve

1 tablespoon chopped roasted peanuts

1 lime, halved

¾oz (20g) bean sprouts

Pad Thai is one of the more difficult noodle dishes to cook. It's not actually that hard but it's got some weird techniques that, if you're a westerner, you may find a bit perplexing. You need to fry the component parts separately and use a wok that is scarily hot. But if you have all of your ingredients at the ready, why is this pimped up? In my youth in Thailand I was taught to make it with ketchup and Maggi liquid seasoning (along with the obligatory tamarind and fish sauce). It's what all the kids were doing and it really made the whole sweet, sour, spicy balance work. I've since visited Thailand and been taught a new way to make it that has the same ethos as what I learned in the nineties, but packs even more of a punch, since it uses California-made Sriracha chili sauce (instead of the ketchup) and oyster sauce, too. Maggi liquid seasoning contains MSG—use it if you want to.

••

Mix together all the ingredients for the pad Thai sauce in a bowl and set aside. You can make a bulk-load of this sauce and keep it in the fridge for up to a month if you like. I've given it to people as presents: better than a box of chocolates if you ask me!

Heat the oil in a wok. When it's REALLY hot, add the strip of tofu and fry it on all sides, being careful not to move it around until it has caramelized and detached itself. Remove from the pan and drain on a paper towel. Cut the strip of tofu into 15–20 slices.

Add the shallot to the wok and fry for 1 minute. Then add the shrimp and cook on both sides until they turn pink. Push the shrimp to one side of the wok and crack in the egg. Quickly scramble the egg in large folds. Throw in the noodles, which will still be firm, then add the chicken stock and stir-fry for 2 minutes. Add the pad Thai sauce and stir-fry for 2 minutes. Return the tofu to the wok, add the salted radish, if using, bean sprouts, and garlic chives and stir-fry for 1 minute more. Serve on a plate with the chopped peanuts, lime, and extra bean sprouts.

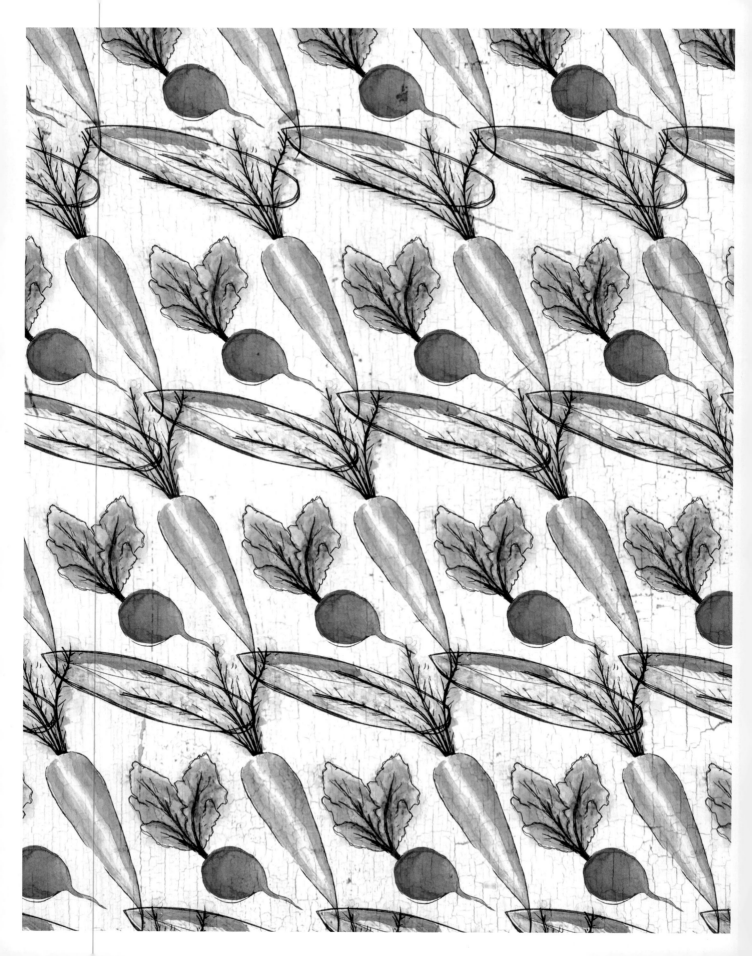

CRUNCH

SALADS & RAW VEGGIES

PREPARATION TIME
5 minutes

COOKING TIME
20 minutes

KALE CHIPS

The first time that I was given kale chips was in a health food store in Los Angeles, where the dehydrated chips were freshly made. I was impressed by how delicious they were, but it wasn't until I tried them baked that I really grasped how good they could be. Kale is one of the best body alkalizers you can get your hands on and it also tastes wonderful. The great thing about kale chips is that they are low carb but taste really naughty, like actual chips, because even a tiny bit of oil will make them crisp up. When you take these out of the oven they will be a little bit soft but in a matter of minutes they will be as crisp as any chip could be and equally as addicting, while also packing a nutritional punch! I've seasoned these simply with nutritional yeast and salt, which gives them a marmitey and almost meaty finish, and the nutritional yeast is full of B vitamins.

Heat the oven to 300°F (150°C). Line 2 large baking trays with parchment paper.

Remove the stems from the kale and roughly tear up the leaves into large pieces. (You can compost the stems or freeze them to use in smoothies.) Wash and thoroughly dry the leaves.

Place the kale leaves in a large bowl and massage the oil into all the nooks and crannies of the leaves until they are thoroughly coated. Now sprinkle with the salt and nutritional yeast. Spread the kale out over the prepared baking trays in a single layer, being careful not to overcrowd them.

Bake for 10 minutes, then rotate the trays and bake for a further 5–10 minutes, or until the kale begins to firm up and shrink a little. Leave the kale to cool on the baking trays for 3 minutes, or until it crisps up. The chips will last for about 2 weeks in a sealed plastic container.

½lb (200g) kale
1 tablespoon olive oil
pinch of salt
1 tablespoon nutritional yeast
  (optional—but the chips do
  taste better with it)

CRUDITÉS

SERVES 6

PREPARATION TIME
15 minutes

COOKING TIME
None

My dream crudités

1 small Lebanese or Persian
  cucumber or ½ regular
  cucumber, deseeded and cut
  into batons
6 radishes with leaves
4 baby carrots
4 cauliflower florets
4 purple cauliflower florets
4 romesco cauliflower florets
4 celery stick tops with leaves
4 asparagus spears, blanched
  for a few seconds and
  refreshed in iced water
4 Little Gem lettuce leaves
4 chicory leaves

Crudités can feel so damn eighties bad buffet party, but when done well, it is one of the most beautiful and delicious ways to show off really great vegetables. A platter overflowing with an array of crunchy vegetables in different colors and shapes looks best, but sometimes simply serving some beautiful radishes, for example, can suffice, since it's the dips as much as the veggies that do the talking. Here are three of my favorite ways (see pages 36–9) to show off crudités. The crudités can be a mixture of any salad vegetables you have to hand, but I've listed my favorites below.

Arrange your crudités neatly on a serving plate and serve with dipping sauces (see pages 36–9).

SOPHIE'S ANCHOVY DIP

SERVES 2 as a snack or as part of a
lunch or appetizer, with enough dip for 6

PREPARATION TIME
10 minutes

COOKING TIME
None

2 garlic cloves, grated
1 tablespoon Dijon mustard
3–4 anchovies in oil, bashed
  into a paste
sea salt flakes and freshly
  ground black pepper
1 tablespoon sherry or white
  wine vinegar
squeeze of lemon juice
2 free-range egg yolks
⅔ cup (150ml) olive oil
⅓ cup (75ml) vegetable oil

The crudités and dip that my friend Sophie Michell serves at her restaurant, Pont St, are the best I've had outside of the south of France. Eat them as a snack, as lunch alongside some cured meat, or as an appetizer.

Pop the garlic, mustard, and anchovy paste into a mixing bowl with plenty of salt and pepper. Add the vinegar, lemon juice, and egg yolks, and then use a small whisk to whisk them together. Slowly whisk in the oils, adding them in a slow thin stream, as if you were making mayonnaise, in order for the sauce to emulsify. If the oil is added too quickly the sauce will either split or not thicken properly. Check the seasoning, and then transfer to a dipping bowl. Keep in the fridge for up to 1 week.

SERVES 6

PREPARATION TIME
10 minutes, plus soaking

COOKING TIME
None

SMOKED SALMON & COD ROE

This is my favorite way to eat crudités. This dip is also my cat Kimchi's favorite human food. It's basically like Greek taramosalata that's been pimped up with smoked salmon to become lighter and a little more moussey, and it's great as a snack served with radishes or crispy fish skin. The method is similar to making a mayonnaise but much easier. Cooking with cod roe may be a new one for you, but if you like store-bought taramosalata then you will love the freshness of making it from scratch.

Before you start, soak the cod roe in a bowl of cold water for at least a couple of hours. Drain it thoroughly, and then peel off the skin.

Put the cod roe in a blender with the garlic and blend it at top speed, gradually pouring in the lemon juice. Start adding the oils a drop at a time (as you would if you were making mayonnaise) and keep adding the oil until the mixture becomes firm. Add the smoked salmon and blend. Gradually pour in just enough boiling water to blend until the mixture becomes a soft mousse. Don't add the water before the mixture has become solid or it will separate. Sprinkle with black onion seeds and serve alongside radishes or mixed crudités.

8oz (225g) smoked cod roe
1 garlic clove, grated
3 tablespoons lemon juice
⅔ cup (150ml) light olive oil
1 cup (250ml) vegetable oil
3½oz (100g) smoked salmon
¼–½ cup (50–100ml) boiling water
black onion seeds, to sprinkle
radishes or Crudités (see opposite)

SERVES 6
....

PREPARATION TIME
10 minutes

COOKING TIME
10 minutes

WALNUT BAGNA CAUDA

This is a recipe for which I have been searching for years. I first tried it at the famous London Italian restaurant San Lorenzo, and it has stuck with me forever.

Traditionally bagna cauda is made as an oil- and butter-based dipping sauce but my mom and I remember it being very walnutty. I researched the recipe and couldn't find a version with walnuts in it anywhere, but I did find some versions using walnut oil. I've totally made up this recipe, but it's pretty damn close to the original and, more importantly, it's delicious.

Heat the olive oil in a saucepan, then add the garlic and fry it very slowly in the oil for about 1–2 minutes, or until the garlic has tinged a little golden. Add the anchovies and let them melt away into the oil. Next, add the walnuts and gently toast them for 1 minute. Add the heavy cream and butter and cook for 2 minutes, or until the mixture is piping hot, and then finish with the walnut oil and lemon juice.

Now you need to blend this to a purée in a small blender. You want it to be the texture of a thin, creamy hummus, almost like a thick, coating-consistency salad dressing. Transfer the bagna cauda to a heatproof pot with a flame underneath (the obvious choice would be a fondue pot) and plunge away at it with your crudités.

⅔ cup (150ml) extra virgin
  olive oil
3–4 garlic cloves, finely
  chopped
8 anchovies
3½oz (100g) walnut halves
  (about 1 cup)
⅔ cup (150ml) heavy cream
2 tablespoons (30g) butter
2 tablespoons walnut oil
1 teaspoon lemon juice
Crudités (see page 36)

PREPARATION TIME
35 minutes, plus marinating

COOKING TIME
5 minutes

PICKLED VEGETABLE PATCH SALAD

Angela Hartnett and Luke Holder have a restaurant at London's 5-star Lime Wood hotel called Hartnett Holder & Co. They grow everything on site and even make their own charcuterie. One of the dishes they do is a BRILLIANT sharing platter that looks just like a vegetable patch, and this is my version of that dish, complete with cheater's olive "soil." The pickled veggies are just awesome on their own but this whole salad platter makes a really cool appetizer or part of a buffet (which, by the way, I'm all about bringing back...).

Melt the vinegar, sugar, salt, thyme, and chili in a saucepan, and then pour over the vegetables in a large non-reactive bowl. Cover with plastic wrap and leave until completely cool—this will take about 2 hours.

To make the olive soil, place the olives in a food processor and pulse. The blitzed olives will be quite wet so lay them on some paper towel and squeeze out the excess liquid. Transfer to a bowl.

Next, blend half the seeds with the salt in a food processor until they're dust. Transfer to a bowl, add the remaining seeds, and mix well.

To serve, mash up and spread the goat curd in a line on the base of a large platter, then spread a line of the olive soil, and finally a line of seeds. Arrange the vegetables in rows on top to make it slightly resemble a vegetable garden. Drizzle with the oil, bring to the table, and scarf straightaway, either by scooping up and plating or just dipping into the elements.

3½oz (100g) pitted black olives

3½oz (100g) toasted mixed seeds (sesame, sunflower, and pumpkin seeds are best)

½ teaspoon salt

10oz (300g) goat cheese curd (or fresh goat cheese/chèvre)

2 tablespoons canola or really good extra virgin olive oil

For the vegetables

2 cups (500ml) white wine or cider vinegar

1 cup (200g) fine organic cane sugar (or granulated sugar)

3 tablespoons table salt

1 thyme sprig

1 small dried chili or a pinch of dried chili flakes

2oz (60g) cauliflower, cut into florets (about 1 cup)

2oz (60g) romanesco cauliflower, cut into florets (about 1 cup)

2oz (60g) purple cauliflower, cut into florets (about 1 cup)

a small bunch of baby carrots, trimmed and tidied

2 baby fennel bulbs, cut in half lengthways

12 radishes with leaves

PREPARATION TIME
30 minutes, plus cooling

COOKING TIME
20 minutes

BHEL PURI SALAD WITH HEIRLOOM TOMATOES

For the date & tamarind chutney

14 dates, pitted
1 tablespoon dried tamarind, rehydrated in 1 cup (250ml) boiling water
1 tablespoon jaggery, palm sugar, or brown sugar
1 teaspoon chat or garam masala
1 teaspoon ground cumin
½ teaspoon red chili powder

For the green chutney dressing

1 small package (30g) of cilantro, leaves picked
a handful of mint leaves
2 green chilies, deseeded if you don't want the dressing to be too spicy
1in (3cm) piece of fresh ginger root, peeled
1 teaspoon cumin seeds, toasted
¼ teaspoon garam masala
3 tablespoons lemon juice
a good pinch of salt

For the salad

1½lb (700g) heirloom tomatoes (a mixture of different colors, varieties, and sizes)
¼ teaspoon table salt, or enough to season your tomatoes
1 red onion, finely chopped
1 cucumber, peeled and finely diced
seeds from 1 pomegranate
1 x 14oz (400g) can chickpeas, drained
a bunch of cilantro, roughly chopped
1¼ cups (30g) Indian puffed rice (this looks like long Rice Krispies)
1¼ cups (60g) plain bhujia (chickpea noodles)

Indian food is just wonderful and so diverse. I was introduced to bhel puri by Horn OK Please, an Indian street-food company. Bhel puri is basically a salad of vegetables and onions mixed with crunchy puffed rice and chickpea noodles (both of which can be bought from Indian supermarkets), a date and tamarind chutney, and a green chutney. It's sweet, sour, spicy, crunchy, fresh, and such a healthy snack. I've used great farm-bought heirloom tomatoes and chickpeas in this recipe and made the dish into a bit more of a salad. If you have any of the chutney left over, serve it with puris or poppadums or alongside curry: for me, it beats mango chutney and raita every time.

To make the date and tamarind chutney, place all the ingredients in a blender and blend together until smooth. It will be a fairly thin chutney but you don't want any lumps in it, so make sure you blend it until it is really smooth. Pour into a saucepan and cook down slowly over lowish heat for 20 minutes, or until the flavors are rich, homogenized, and cooked out and the chutney has thickened to the consistency of a thick ketchup. Set aside to cool.

To make the green chutney dressing, place all the ingredients in a small blender and whiz until it is a smooth paste. Set aside.

Now you need to get on with making your salad. Cut the tomatoes into a variety of different shapes and sizes and place in a bowl with the salt. Add all the remaining salad ingredients except for the puffed rice and bhujia. Pour on the date and tamarind chutney and the green chutney dressing and mix thoroughly. Next, add two-thirds of the puffed rice and bhujia and mix quickly—the salad will make popping noises, just like when you add milk to Rice Krispies.

To serve, divide the salad between 4 plates, and then sprinkle over the remaining puffed rice and bhujia. Eat straightaway so that the crispy ingredients don't get soggy!

SERVES 4
....

PREPARATION TIME
20 minutes, plus soaking

COOKING TIME
None

AVOCADO SALAD WITH WASABI, WAKAME & SCALLIONS

Avocado is not a traditional Japanese ingredient, though we do associate it with Japanese cuisine due to the brilliant Japanese fusion food that comes out of California. Avocado just works so well with Japanese flavors. This salad also includes wasabi, which is Japanese horseradish, for those of you still living in the Dark Ages, and wakame, which is dried and then rehydrated seaweed. This healthy salad is delicious on its own and is also great served alongside teriyaki or miso fish.

....

Place the wakame in a heatproof bowl and cover with boiling water. Leave to soak for 15 minutes. The wakame will rehydrate and grow in size, so cover with plenty of water to allow for this. It's ready when it has doubled in size and you can bite through it but it still has chew. Drain, and then rinse under cold running water to cool. Alternatively, you can cool the wakame in a bowl of iced water. Drain again and gently pat dry with paper towel.

To make the dressing, place the wasabi, vinegar, oils, and some salt and pepper in a bowl and whisk together until it has fully emulsified into a thickish sauce.

Cut the avocados in half, remove the pits, and then peel off the skins. Slice the halved avocados and place on a platter. Once you've done this, gently press the top of the avocados to fan out the slices a little. Top with the dressing, then the wakame, then the radishes, then the scallions, and finally sprinkle with the sesame seeds. Serve straightaway.

1oz (25g) dried wakame seaweed
4 ripe but firm avocados
10 pink radishes, very thinly sliced
6 scallions, finely chopped
1 tablespoon black sesame seeds, toasted
1 tablespoon white sesame seeds, toasted

For the dressing

3 teaspoons wasabi paste (use the best you can find)
¼ cup (60ml) rice wine vinegar
¼ cup (60ml) light olive oil
2 tablespoons sesame oil
sea salt flakes and freshly ground black pepper

SERVES 4

PREPARATION TIME
20 minutes

COOKING TIME
10 minutes

CEVICHE WITH YUZU, SESAME & KUMQUATS

The first time that I had ceviche was when I was 21 years old and on a beach in Tulum, Mexico. When I was younger, I was a bit freaked about eating sushi and the idea of eating raw fish that had been macerated in lime juice (which is essentially what ceviche is) made me feel much the same. I can't tell you how it works exactly but the citrus juice cooks the fish and I mean COOKS it. If you leave your ceviche to macerate for long enough the fish will be cooked all the way through. In fact, you're curing the fish at the same time as you're marinating it. This process also gives the fish tons of flavor. A lot of Latin American coastal countries claim ceviche as their own. It's a classic Peruvian dish and if there is one thing I know about Peruvian cuisine it's that it is a mishmash of many cultures: genuine fusion food. Martin Morales, from the restaurant Ceviche, once told me that there are no rules in Peruvian cooking and this gives him free rein to play with his food. Martin has used passion fruit and pomegranate in his ceviche; both are acidic fruits with a different tang that work brilliantly with the fish. I love Japanese fusion food, so here I've combined yuzu and sesame (the flavors from my favorite sashimi dish) with kumquats, the tiny citrus fruits that have an acidic flesh and super-sweet skins. And what do you know? It's a triumph!

1 large wild sea bass, about 1¾lb–2lb (800g–1kg), filleted and skinned
1 corn on the cob, husk removed
olive oil
1 large ripe avocado, peeled, pitted, and cut into small cubes
6 kumquats, thinly sliced horizontally into 6 or 7 pieces and seeded
½ large red onion, very thinly sliced
a few cilantro leaves, roughly chopped

For the "tiger's milk"
1 garlic clove, finely grated
1 large hot red chili or 2 small ones, deseeded and finely chopped
¾ teaspoon salt
¼ cup (60ml) yuzu juice
2 tablespoons soy sauce
2 tablespoons sesame oil

Cut the fish into thick slices of sashimi, about ⅙in (4mm) thick. Put the slices in a mixing bowl, cover with plastic wrap, and place in the fridge. I do this first, since it's good to have all the ingredients ready to go when the time comes to construct the dish.

Next, heat a grill pan until it's smoking. Rub the corn with some oil, and then grill it on all sides until it's charred all over but the corn is still firm. Remove from the heat and leave to cool for 5 minutes. Then, using a sharp knife, carve off the corn kernels and place them in a bowl with the avocado and kumquats.

To make the "tiger's milk," pound together the garlic, chili pepper, and salt using a large mortar and pestle, slowly trickling in the yuzu juice, soy sauce, and sesame oil.

"Tigers milk" is the sauce that's used to dress the ceviche. When you mix the sauce with the fish it goes a little milky from the protein.

Once you're ready to rock-and-roll, add the red onion and the "tiger's milk" to a non-reactive bowl, add the fish, and give it a good stir. Throw it back in the fridge and leave for 5 minutes. I like my fish to still be a little raw in the middle but if you prefer your fish to be more "cooked" then you can leave it in the fridge for up to 20 minutes. Next, add the corn, avocado, kumquats, and cilantro to the bowl and give it another good stir to combine. Leave for a further 5 minutes, then stir again and serve straightaway. Some people serve ceviche in glasses or alongside a small fried corn tortilla or with tortilla chips, so feel free to go to town if you want to.

SERVES 4

....

PREPARATION TIME

30 minutes, plus drying
overnight

COOKING TIME

1½ hours

THAI ROAST DUCK &
WATERMELON SALAD

8½ cups (2 liters) water
1 star anise
1 slice of galangal or ginger,
  bruised
2 scallions, split down the
  middle
5 tablespoons maltose or
  (if you really can't find it)
  honey
¼ cup (60ml) light soy sauce
2 tablespoons salt
1 free-range duck, about 3–7lb
  (1.4–3kg), not too fatty
Thai Salad Dressing (see
  opposite)
lime wedges, to serve

For the salad

½ medium watermelon, cut into
  small cubes
3½oz (100g) cashews or peanuts,
  roasted
a small handful of Thai basil
  leaves
a small handful of mint leaves
a small handful of cilantro
  leaves
1 shallot, finely sliced
Crispy Shallots (see page 79)

You will also need a saucepan
  large enough to fit the
  whole duck

One of my most memorable cooking experiences was when I worked at Min Jiang at the Royal Garden Hotel in Kensington, which is famous for its roast duck and dim sum. I spent a day learning all the secrets to the perfect Crispy Peking Duck. It's no mean feat. First, air is blown under the duck's skin to separate the skin from the flesh. The duck is doused in searing hot syrup to constrict and glaze the skin, then it is left to dry overnight. It's then roasted at a really hot temperature and actually served pink. The skin is carved away and the duck is sliced rather than shredded and served with plum sauce, scallions, cucumber, and pancakes. I've made my recipe a bit more user-friendly. Essentially, you are just giving the duck a hot bath in molten liquor for a few minutes before drying it out in the fridge overnight and then roasting it. It's no more effort than marinating something the night before, just a little more unusual. I've paired the duck with the most deelish Thai watermelon salad, inspired by chef Ian Pengelley, but feel free to serve the duck the classic way with pancakes if you prefer.

....

Place the water, star anise, galangal or ginger, scallions, maltose or honey, soy sauce, and salt in the large saucepan and bring to a boil. Turn off the heat and leave to infuse for 10 minutes. Bring back to a boil, scoop out the aromatics, and then plunge the duck, skin-side up, into the water and immerse it fully. You may need to keep it pushed down with a wooden spoon. Bring to a boil for 3 minutes, then quickly remove the duck and dry fully on paper towel.

Clear a shelf in the fridge, lay a few sheets of plastic wrap on the shelf, and then place some paper towel on top. Next, lay a wire rack on top of this. Place the duck on the wire rack and leave to dry in the fridge for 15 hours. The duck skin will feel like wax paper when it's dry.

Preheat the oven to 400°F (200°C). Place the duck on a rack in a roasting pan and fill the pan with 1¼ cups (300ml) water. If you want classic roast Chinese duck that's still pink, roast the duck for 40 minutes, or until the skin is crisp and golden;

if you want crispy duck, cook for 60 minutes, turning the oven down to 350°F (180°C) after 30 minutes. Leave the duck to rest for 10 minutes before carving. Carve off the legs and use two forks to shred the leg meat, removing the bones as you go. Next, if you're serving your duck pink, remove the breasts with the skin intact and cut widthways into slices; or you can shred it like the legs. Sprinkle with a tiny bit of salt, then arrange on one side of a large serving platter.

Place the watermelon on the platter and scatter with the nuts, herbs, shallot slices, and Crispy Shallots. Serve with the Thai Salad Dressing and lime wedges.

THAI SALAD DRESSING

SERVES 4

⅔ cup (150ml) water
200g palm sugar
3–4 Thai red chilies, sliced
1 lemongrass stick, bruised
1 small piece of galangal or
  fresh ginger, about 2in x
  1in (5cm x 2.5cm), bruised
5 lime leaves, torn
2 tablespoons tamarind paste
2 tablespoons fish sauce
2 tablespoons lime juice

Boil all the ingredients together in a saucepan over medium heat for about 5 minutes, or until it has reduced and is like honey. It needs to be thicker and more potent than your average dressing because it will be diluted with all the juice the watermelon lets out. Leave to cool.

SUPERFOOD SALAD

This salad has everything you could possibly want for health: oily fish for brain development and building a good heart, and a variety of green vegetables for balancing alkalinity in the blood. Kale is a winner in salads but you need to give it a really quick blanch first or it can be like eating tickly autumn leaves. The avocado is full of vitamin E and good oils that will help you burn fat, and it's the same deal with the seeds. There's quinoa for carbs and more protein, and we're toasting it to give it a more nutty flavor. The Japanese dressing with shallots and ginger will cleanse your blood and give it some spunk.

··

½ cup (100g) quinoa
¼lb (115g) kale, blanched for 30 seconds and refreshed in iced water
3½oz (100g) fresh or frozen edamame beans
½ head of broccoli, cut into small florets
1 avocado, peeled, pitted, and chopped
2 scallions, thinly sliced
10 radishes, thinly sliced
about ¾lb (340g) perfectly cooked or hot-smoked salmon, skin removed and flesh flaked
1 tablespoon toasted black and/or white sesame seeds

For the Japanese salad dressing

1 banana shallot, very finely chopped
1in (3cm) piece of fresh ginger root, peeled and grated
6 tablespoons rice wine vinegar
6 tablespoons soy sauce
6 tablespoons sesame oil
sea salt flakes and freshly ground black pepper

Put the quinoa in a dry frying pan and toast over medium heat, keeping the quinoa moving the whole time, until it's lightly golden and nutty. Transfer to a small saucepan and add a good pinch of salt and 1⅓ cups (320ml) water. Cover, bring to a boil, and cook for 10 minutes. Remove from the heat and, keeping the lid on, let the quinoa steam for 5 minutes to soak up the remaining liquid and get fluffy.

To make the dressing, place all the ingredients in a clean jam jar and season with salt and pepper. Screw the lid on tightly and shake it like crazy.

Drain the kale and dry it on paper towel, then roughly chop. Place the kale in a large salad bowl along with the edamame beans, broccoli, avocado, scallions, radishes, and quinoa. Dress with two-thirds of the salad dressing, give a swift mix so as not to let the avocado break up too much, then divide between 4 plates. Top with the salmon and the remaining dressing and finish with a scattering of the sesame seeds.

GRILLED MARINATED WHOLE CHICKEN CAESAR SALAD

I'm not really a salad kinda gal. I like food that's a bit more buxom. I need to have a major protein hit if I'm going to really enjoy my food, and the balance in most salads isn't quite right. Chicken salads piss me off. Mostly because they are made with chicken breasts and I prefer my meat on the bone but also because they're built to be quite delicate. I'm 5ft 10in and a broad-shouldered tomboy, certainly not delicate. The flavors of Caesar salad fit my brief: Parmesan, anchovy, and garlic all smack you round the chops. It's a good salad. But it's a better salad when served alongside a whole grilled chicken.

1 medium free-range chicken, spatchcocked
1 bulb of garlic, cloves peeled and finely chopped
3 tablespoons chopped herbs (I would go for thyme, rosemary, and parsley)
2 tablespoons Korean or regular chili powder
1 teaspoon sea salt flakes
freshly ground black pepper
zest and juice of 1 lemon
2 tablespoons olive oil

For the croutons

scant ½ cup (100ml) olive oil
4 garlic cloves, bashed
2 rosemary sprigs
¼ white loaf or white sourdough bread, trimmed of crusts and torn into bite-sized pieces

For the salad

2 Romaine lettuces or 4 Little Gem lettuces, sliced
Light Caesar Dressing (see opposite)
4 free-range eggs (I like to use pasture-raised), soft-boiled for 6 minutes
8 pickled anchovies, sliced in half lengthways
1oz (30g) Parmesan cheese, shaved

Lay the spatchcocked chicken in a roasting tray. Using a mortar and pestle, bash together the garlic, herbs, chili, salt and pepper, and lemon zest, gradually adding the lemon juice and oil. Rub this marinade all over the chicken, cover with plastic wrap, and leave in the fridge overnight to marinate.

To make the croutons, preheat the oven to 350°F (180°C). Place the oil, garlic, and rosemary in a saucepan and heat until the garlic and herbs start to sizzle. Remove from the heat and leave to stand for 10 minutes. Strain the garlic and herbs from the oil and set both the infused oil and the garlic and herbs aside. Lay the bread in a roasting pan and drizzle with the infused oil. Roast for 25 minutes, turning the croutons halfway through, until golden on the outside. I don't like dried out croutons; I prefer them to have a bit of give in the middle.

Heat a grill pan until smoking and cook the chicken on each side until lightly charred. Return the chicken to the roasting pan and cook in the oven for 25 minutes, or until the juices in the legs run clear. Chop the chicken through its joints into 10 pieces.

Throw the lettuce leaves into a bowl and coat with half of the dressing. Place the leaves on a platter and pour the other half of the dressing over them. Cut the boiled eggs in half and place on top, along with the anchovies, Parmesan shavings, and reserved crispy rosemary sprigs and croutons. Serve alongside the chicken with the chicken juices poured over.

LIGHT CAESAR DRESSING

My girly addition to this recipe is the salad dressing, which I've made much lighter by using less oil and replacing some of the oil with plain yogurt. The tang of the yogurt is great with the vinegar and it cuts down the calories. So I might be a tomboy but my butt likes me to remember to keep myself in check!

SERVES 4-6

1 egg yolk
5 anchovies in oil
1 teaspoon Dijon mustard
1 tablespoon white wine
  vinegar
1¾oz (50g) Parmesan cheese,
  grated
2 garlic cloves (you can use
  the cooked leftover garlic
  from making the croutons)
scant 1 cup (200ml) light
  olive oil
scant ½ cup (100g) plain yogurt
juice of 1 lemon
sea salt flakes and freshly
  ground black pepper

Put the egg yolk, anchovies, mustard, vinegar, Parmesan, and garlic cloves in a food processor and blend until smooth. Continue to blend and slowly trickle in the oil until the dressing thickens up. Mix in the yogurt and season with the lemon juice and salt and pepper.

SOFIA'S PINKALILLI

MAKES 4–6 pint (450g) jars
....

PREPARATION TIME
25 minutes, plus 2 hours
salting

COOKING TIME
40 minutes

I have a sidekick who helps me with everything. Her name is Sofia. I couldn't do what I do without her. She is a beautiful girl in her mid-twenties from Sweden, but don't let her looks fool you—this girl is a powerhouse. I dread the day she wants to leave me. I asked her to contribute a recipe to the book, and knowing me so well she went with a classic recipe but made it hot pink. So here we have Sofia's pinkalilli recipe. It's based on a classic piccalilli but made with beet. Serve it with cold roast pork or cured meats—basically anything porky.

½lb (200g) beets, peeled and cut into bite-sized pieces (keeping the peel)

2½ cups (600ml) white wine vinegar

5oz (150g) runner beans (Romano beans), trimmed and cut into ½in (1cm) or bite-sized pieces

5oz (150g) string beans, each trimmed and cut into 4 pieces

½ large cauliflower, cut into small florets

2 zucchini, cut into ½in (1cm) or bite-sized pieces

7oz (200g) frozen peeled pearl onions, defrosted

1½ tablespoons table salt

3 baby cucumbers, deseeded and cut into 1cm or bite-sized pieces

1 bay leaf

1½ teaspoons mustard seeds

2 garlic cloves, crushed

1in (3cm) piece of fresh ginger root, peeled and grated

¾ cup (150g) fine organic cane sugar (or granulated sugar)

1 tablespoon English mustard powder

1 tablespoon all-purpose flour

1 teaspoon cornstarch

Put the beet peel and vinegar in a non-reactive bowl and set aside.

Lay the runner beans, string beans, cauliflower, zucchini, and onions in a colander and sprinkle with most of the salt, reserving ½ tablespoon of salt for the cucumber, and set aside for 2 hours. For the final 30 minutes, lay the cucumber in a separate colander and sprinkle with the reserved salt.

Rinse the vegetables well and drain. Put the runner beans, string beans, cauliflower, zucchini, onions, and beet in a large Dutch oven.

Remove the beet peel from the vinegar and discard. Add the vinegar to the pot, together with the bay leaf, mustard seeds, garlic, and ginger. Bring to a simmer and cook gently until the vegetables are just beginning to soften but still have a bite to them. Add the cucumber and sugar and cook for 3–4 minutes. Set a large colander over a bowl, strain the vegetables, and then pour the vinegar liquor into a measuring jug.

In a large saucepan, mix together the mustard powder, flour, and cornstarch, add about 3 tablespoons of the vinegar liquor, and whisk until smooth, then stir in the rest of the liquor. Set the pan over medium heat and cook, stirring all the time, until the sauce starts to thicken. Cook gently for about 8–10 minutes, or until the sauce has the consistency of thick cream. Add the vegetables to the sauce and mix well.

Transfer to 4–6 sterilized jars and allow to cool before sealing tightly. Store in the fridge and use within 1 month.

TOASTED BLACK SESAME BUTTER

Black sesame butter sounds like a revelation but has been used in Asian cooking for years. It's the base of a lot of Korean and Japanese dishes, and I've been using it for everything from ice cream to Korean rice porridge (juk). I started making my own when I became obsessed with making different-flavored nut butters. I tested them on apples and bits of crackers, and I started to get a taste for this one as a kind of butter rather than the simple sesame paste it was known for. I added a touch of sweetness and some salt. Now it's fully addictive straight from the jar and eaten in the same way as you would peanut butter, but also in dressings and as a tahini in dips. It may look like tar and taste like it's utterly filthy for you, but those little black sesame seeds are high in protein, packed with virtually every mineral there is, and great for reducing cholesterol. It tastes damn good too.

Place the sesame seeds in a dry pan and toast them over low heat for about 5 minutes. It's hard to tell with black sesame seeds when they are toasted but you need to judge with your nose. It's important they are well toasted, otherwise the butter will taste a little bitter and raw, but be careful not to burn them.

Place these in a high-power food processor and whiz until the seeds have broken up. Next add the oil, maple syrup, and salt and blend for at least 30 seconds, or until fully blended. Transfer into a sterilized jar and seal firmly. This will last for weeks if you can avoid guzzling it all.

3½oz (100g) black sesame seeds
4-5 tablespoons sesame oil
   (NOT TOASTED) or vegetable oil
1 tablespoon maple syrup
a good pinch of sea salt flakes

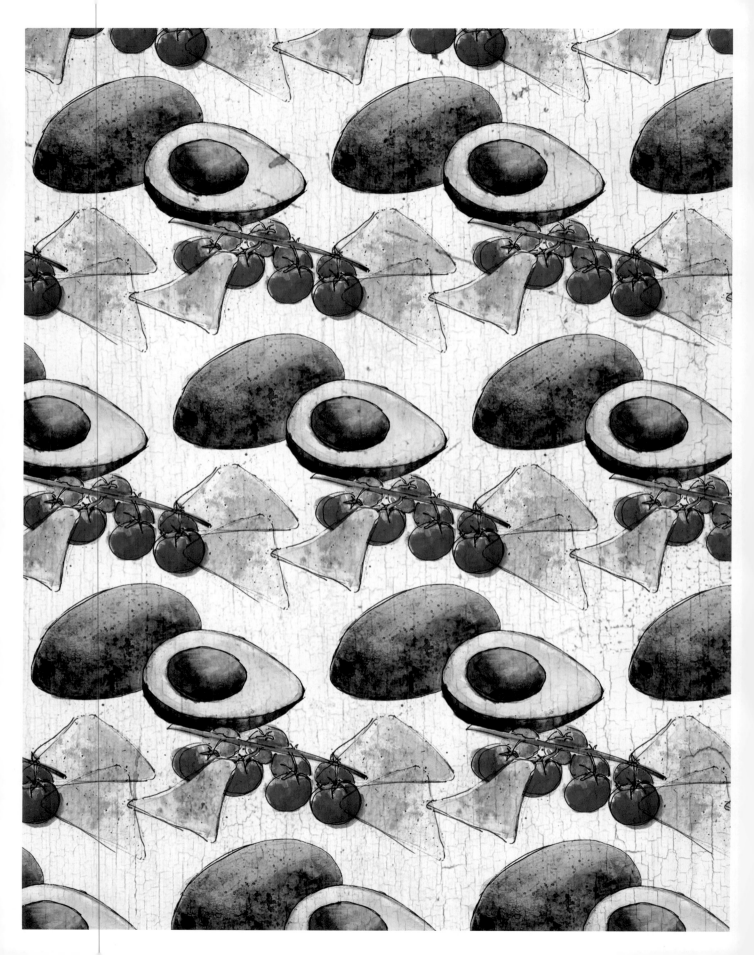

CRISP

FRIED & CRUMBED

CHOPPED LIVER WITH EGG & GRIBENES

Chopped liver is like a coarse pâté. Traditionally, it's made by frying chicken livers with onions, hand-chopping them, and then mixing them with schmaltz. I have taken some French pâté-making techniques and used them to make pâté's Jewish brother, slowly cooking shallots with port and Madeira to add sweetness and body to complement the livers before whizzing them in a blender to a still-rough but slightly smoother texture.

....

¾lb (350g) chicken livers
sea salt flakes and freshly
  ground black pepper
⅔ cup (150ml) Schmaltz
  (see page 216)
3 large shallots, finely
  chopped
a few thyme sprigs
2 tablespoons Madeira
2 tablespoons port
generous grating of nutmeg

To serve

2 hard-boiled free-range eggs
  (I like pasture-raised, since
  they have orange yolks),
  grated
3½oz (100g) Gribenes (see
  page 216)
1 tablespoon finely chopped
  parsley
a few dill sprigs
toasted challah or matzo
  crackers
dill pickles and/or new green
  pickles, sliced

Prepare the chicken livers by removing the vascular centers carefully with a knife. Season with plenty of salt and pepper.

Heat 2 tablespoons of schmaltz in a frying pan. When hot, add the chicken livers and fry until brown on all sides. You need to make sure that the livers are cooked through but still very pink in the middles or the finished dish will be grey rather than the parfait pink that you want it to be. Set the livers aside on a plate.

Wipe the pan clean with a paper towel to remove any scorched bits, then add 3 more tablespoons of schmaltz to the pan. Add the shallots and thyme and fry over a lower heat for about 5 minutes, or until they have softened enough that you can squash them with your fingertips. Pour in the Madeira and port, bring to a boil, and cook for 1–2 minutes, or until the liquid has disappeared and the shallots are bright pink. Remove the thyme and set aside to cool for 10 minutes.

Put the livers, shallots, the remaining schmaltz, nutmeg, and some salt and pepper in a food processor. Pulse until the mixture forms a rough pâté-like paste. Transfer to a terrine or plastic container and top with wax paper to stop the surface oxidizing. Wrap the terrine or container tightly with plastic wrap and refrigerate overnight.

Remove the pâté from the fridge 10 minutes before serving. Unwrap the terrine or container and heat 2 serving spoons in boiling water. Dry the spoons and use them to make a quenelle (a ball) of pâté to place on each plate. Sprinkle some grated egg, Gribenes, and herbs over the top of each quenelle and serve with matzo crackers or toasted challah and some pickles.

POTATO LATKES

Latkes remind me of going to NYC with my manager, who is like my big sister, and eating the hugest salt-beef sandwiches, bowls of chicken noodle soup, chopped liver, egg, and onions, and latkes with sour cream. I ended up smearing the latkes with everything served at the dinner table. I love latkes—they are like rösti but better. I love them served with cream cheese and smoked salmon for breakfast, or with fried eggs, or with... basically anything!

Heat the butter in frying pan over medium heat and fry the onion for 10 minutes, or until softened. Set aside.

Grate the potatoes on the coarse holes of a grater, then transfer the grated potatoes to a large colander set over a large bowl. Squeeze the water out of the potatoes, letting the liquid drip through the holes of the colander into the bowl. Let this liquid sit in the bowl for a few minutes, then carefully pour out the water but keep the layer of pale beige paste at the bottom of the bowl. This is potato starch, which will help your latkes stick together.

Add the potatoes, onion, egg yolks, matzo meal, and salt to the potato starch and give it all a good mix until everything is evenly incorporated.

Preheat the oven to 350°F (180°C).

In a separate, spotlessly clean bowl, whisk the egg whites until stiff, then fold them into the potato mixture.

Heat 2 tablespoons of oil in a frying pan, then spoon a couple of tablespoons of the potato mixture into the pan and fry for few minutes on each side, or until the latkes are nice and golden. Repeat until you have used up all the mixture. Transfer the finished latkes to a baking sheet and bake for 15 minutes, or until they are all cooked through. Serve with sour cream or cream cheese and season with black pepper.

1 tablespoon butter
1 large onion, finely chopped
6 large russet potatoes, scrubbed
2 free-range eggs, separated
2 tablespoons matzo meal
2 teaspoons salt
corn or vegetable oil, for frying
sour cream or cream cheese, to serve
freshly grated black pepper

SERVES 4 as an appetizer
or 2-4 when watching a movie

PREPARATION TIME
20 minutes

COOKING TIME
35 minutes

NACHOS WITH REFRIED BEANS

My best night in ever is watching a good horror movie and having my fill of chips and dips. And the best way to have chips and dips is with loaded nachos. I prefer my nachos with refried beans instead of chili con carne—and it's not often you'll see me choose veggies over meat. Making your own refried beans is easy and so much tastier than the store-bought options. I've used pinto beans, since they are classic, but the recipe works well with red kidney and black beans too. You'll have extra salsa.

5oz (150g) plain tortilla chips
3½oz (100g) Cheddar cheese, grated
Guacamole (see opposite)
⅓ cup (80g) sour cream
3 tablespoons sliced pickled jalepeños
cilantro leaves, to garnish

For the salsa

3-4 tomatoes, deseeded and finely chopped
1 red chili, deseeded and finely chopped
1 garlic clove, grated
juice of 1 large, juicy lime
½ teaspoon sea salt flakes
½ tablespoon extra virgin olive oil

For the refried beans

4 tablespoons lard or (even better) bacon fat, or use any cooking oil you like
1 onion, finely chopped
6 garlic cloves, finely chopped
1 tablespoon cumin seeds
1 teaspoon ground coriander
1 x 14oz (400g) can pinto beans, drained and washed
1¼ cups (300ml) fresh White Chicken or Veggie Stock (see pages 212–13)
sea salt flakes and freshly ground black pepper

Make the salsa by mixing together the tomatoes, chili, garlic, lime juice, salt, and olive oil in a bowl. Set aside to macerate while you make the rest of the dish. By the time you get to use the salsa it will be really watery: that's the salt taking the water out of the tomatoes. Drain off this water but don't throw it away or I will hunt you down! Drink it—it's pure essence of tomato and the yummiest thing on the planet.

To make the refried beans, heat the lard, fat, or oil in a frying pan. Add the onion and fry slowly for about 10 minutes, or until soft and lightly golden, adding the garlic and cumin seeds during the final 1-2 minutes. Add the ground coriander and fry for a further 30 seconds. Add the beans, stir to coat with the oniony spices, and then pour in the stock. Bring to a gentle boil, then reduce the heat and cook over low heat for 10 minutes. When there are only about 3 tablespoons of the liquid left, blend the beans in a food processor until smooth. Wipe the frying pan clean and then return the beans to the pan (you may need a touch more lard, fat, or oil when doing this, depending on how nonstick your pan is). Fry the beans for about 5 minutes or until they change color and thicken up (they should be like a thick hummus). Season to taste with plenty of salt and pepper.

Preheat the oven to 400°F (200°C).

Place the tortilla chips in an ovenproof dish and top with the cheese. Bake them for 10 minutes, or until the cheese has melted. Remove from the oven and top with a layer of the hot refried beans—it looks like a ton but I swear you need it all. Next, top this with a good couple of spoonfuls of guacamole, then the same amount of salsa and the same amount of sour cream. Sprinkle with the jalepeños, garnish with cilantro, and you're good to go!

GUACAMOLE

SERVES 2-4
....

2 very ripe avocados, skins and stones removed
juice of 1 large lime
1 chili, deseeded (unless you like it spicy) and finely chopped
1 garlic clove, grated
pinch of ground cumin
1 large ripe tomato, deseeded and finely chopped
2 scallions, finely sliced
sea salt flakes and freshly ground black pepper

To make the guacamole, mash the avocado in a mortar with a pestle or in a bowl with a fork. Mix in the lime juice, chili, garlic, ground cumin, tomato, and scallions and season with salt and pepper. Lay some plastic wrap over the top of the guacamole and set aside.

PREPARATION TIME
10 minutes

COOKING TIME
20 minutes

KOREAN FRIED CHICKEN

scant 1 cup (200ml) buttermilk
1 tablespoon salt
8 free-range or organic chicken
  wings, wing tips cut off,
  then each wing cut in half
  through the joint to make
  16 pieces
oil, for deep-frying
2 tablespoons toasted sesame
  seeds (white, black, or a
  mixture of both)
2 scallions, (green parts
  only), very thinly sliced
  into rings, to garnish

For the sauce

2 tablespoons gochujang
  (Korean chili paste)
2 tablespoons Sriracha chili
  sauce
¼ cup (50g) sugar
¼ cup (60ml) rice wine vinegar
2 tablespoons ketchup
1 tablespoon sesame oil
1 tablespoon chicken fat or
  butter

For the flour mix

6 tablespoons self-rising flour
3 tablespoons rice flour
3 tablespoons potato flour
sea salt flakes and white
  pepper

This is a recipe that I have made a thousand times and developed over the past six years, having first tried them in K-town in New York at the advice of my friend, chef Judy Joo. It's now (I guess) my "signature dish" and it makes an appearance at pretty much every event, take-over, or pop-up that I do, though I've never fully published it until now. I am writing this recipe while in Seoul and for the first time I feel that I can finally put it to bed, after having eaten mountains of Korean fried chicken from its motherland and knowing for sure that I now have it right. My recipe is a fusion of American meets Asian, brining the wings first to tenderize, season, and firm up the wings then tossing them in three flours. You might think this step is a bit extreme but each flour does its own thing: the self-rising (wheat) flour is for puff, the potato flour is for chew, and the rice flour gives it crunch. Don't mess about with this step. The wings are then fried over low heat until cooked, dried, and then flash-fried on high, making them crisp and drawing out the juices to form an umami crust. Finally, they are tossed in an addictive Korean chili sauce to coat the wings, then in sesame seeds, and garnished with very finely sliced scallions. Serve them the Korean way, piled into mountains alongside a stack of imported beer while watching soccer or K-pop with pals.

....

Mix the buttermilk and salt together in a bowl. Add the chicken wings and massage the brine into the wings, then leave in the fridge for 12–24 hours. This will draw out all the excess water from the wings, leaving the concentrated chicken juices.

To make the sauce, melt together the gochujang, chili sauce, sugar, vinegar, ketchup, sesame oil, and chicken fat or butter in a saucepan. Bring to a boil for a minute, then remove from the heat and set aside.

Mix all the flours together in a bowl and season well. Take the wings out of the buttermilk brine, wiping off any excess with paper towel. Toss the wings, 4 pieces at a time, in the flours. Remove and set aside.

Heat the oil in a deep-fryer (or a deep saucepan or wok filled with oil a third of the way up its sides) to 275°F (140°C). Add the wings and fry gently (or confit) for 8–10 minutes, or until they are cooked through but have barely taken on any color. Remove the wings and drain on paper towel. Increase the temperature of the oil to 375°F (190°C) and fry the wings for a further 2–3 minutes, or until they are golden and cooked through.

Toss the wings in the sauce and 1 tablespoon of the sesame seeds. Sprinkle with the remaining sesame seeds and the scallions and serve immediately. These are best eaten with your fingers and served with an ice-cold beer.

WET & WILD GARLIC CHICKEN KIEVS

Chicken Kievs are utterly delicious—I am squealing inside while I write this recipe and wait for them to cook. Garlic butter makes everything taste good and so does frying anything in breadcrumbs, so here we have a double whammy of deliciousness. Chicken Kievs are a little complicated to make (they must be sealed well, the butter needs to be frozen, and you have to make sure you slit the chicken evenly so that the butter can't seep out) but it's a fun process and a good one to get your hands dirty with. I've pimped up my recipe by roasting fresh wild garlic and then adding this, plus some grated garlic AND some wild garlic, to the butter and then wrapping it in wild garlic leaves. And these chicken Kievs are—I can say this because I've just tasted them—possibly the best thing I've ever eaten. You can quote me on that.

....

16 wild garlic leaves
Garlic Butter (see opposite)
¾ cup (100g) all-purpose flour, seasoned with salt and pepper
2 large free-range eggs, beaten with a little milk
3-4 cups (300g) panko breadcrumbs
4 large free-range chicken breasts with fillets attached (I like using supremes, which you can get from your butcher, since they still have the wing tip attached)
oil, for deep-frying

Take the whole wild garlic leaves and lay them out flat, 4 leaves per chicken breast. Divide the butter between the 4 sets of leaves and roll them up to make 4 parcels about the size and shape of your thumb. Wrap the parcels in plastic wrap and then place them in the freezer for 20–30 minutes, or until they are very firm. (If I have any excess butter, I melt it and serve it poured over the cooked chicken Kievs.)

When the butter is hard, take 3 bowls and fill one with the seasoned flour, one with the beaten eggs, and one with the breadcrumbs. Using a sharp knife, make a deep cut lengthways along each chicken breast to make a pocket in the chicken. Stick your finger in the pocket and root around a bit to make the hole a little bit larger. Unwrap the plastic wrap from the frozen butter parcels and stuff each breast with one of the parcels. Plug up the hole in each chicken breast with the false fillet, or a bit of the false fillet, and pinch the end of the chicken shut.

Lower the oven temperature to 375°F (190°C). Heat the oil in either a deep-fryer or a deep saucepan to 375°F (190°C). Carefully dip each stuffed breast, first in the seasoned flour, then in plenty of the egg, and then in the breadcrumbs, coating them thoroughly and paying particular attention to the end where they've been sealed. I would double-coat the end with more egg and breadcrumbs.

Carefully place each chicken Kiev into the hot oil and cook for 4–5 minutes, or until the Kievs turn a light golden color. Transfer to a baking tray and bake for 12–15 minutes, until cooked through and nicely crisp and brown. Some of the butter will have leaked out, so be sure to pour that back over the chicken when you serve it. Serve the chicken Kievs with mashed potatoes, peas, and any excess butter poured over.

GARLIC BUTTER

SERVES 4

1 bulb of wet garlic
2 wet or dried garlic cloves, grated
Just under 2 sticks (200g) unsalted butter, at room temperature
2 wild garlic leaves, finely sliced, and garlic flowers (if you can find them)
2–3 tablespoons chopped parsley
sea salt flakes and freshly ground black pepper

Heat the oven to 400°F (200°C). Wrap the bulb of wet garlic in foil and roast for 40 minutes, or until the cloves are soft and gooey when squished. Leave to cool a little. Place the squeezed-out roasted garlic cloves in a small food processor with the grated garlic, butter, sliced wild garlic leaves, parsley, and plenty of salt and pepper and process until smooth. If you have managed to get hold of wild garlic flowers, stir them into the garlic butter.

CRISPY CHICKEN, SATAY SAUCE & ASIAN SPIRALIZED VEGETABLE NOODLE SALAD

So now we get to spiralizing vegetables: the art of turning vegetables into "noodles" with a spiralizer. This is a technique that the Japanese have been using for ages to create garnishes, and one that health freaks are now using as a replacement for noodles. Ultimately, you are eating not noodles but salad. I tested cooking spiralized vegetables in a variety of different styles and discovered that even a second of cooking takes the vegetables a little too far, so the best way to eat them is raw with a hot sauce or, even better, marinated. Here, I've taken classic Malay flavors (chili, crispy shallots, fresh herbs, and peanut sauce) and paired them with a variety of different vegetable noodles and some crispy chicken. The result is a dish that's so damn delicious that even though technically you're not eating noodles, you don't feel like you're missing out.

···

6 free-range, skin-on, boneless chicken thighs (if you can't find boneless chicken thighs with the skin on, it is really easy to take the bones out yourself)
2 tablespoons curry powder
pinch of salt
1 tablespoon coconut or canola oil
Crispy Shallots (see opposite)
lime halves, to serve (optional)

For the vegetable noodles

1 large sweet potato, unpeeled
½ daikon radish
1 large zucchini
3 shallots, finely sliced
a large bunch of mint, leaves picked and roughly chopped
a bunch of cilantro, leaves picked and roughly chopped
a bunch of Thai basil leaves (or plain basil if you can't get it), leaves picked and roughly chopped

For the dressing

2 red Thai bird's eye chilies, deseeded if you prefer
juice of 2–3 limes
2 tablespoons fish sauce
1 tablespoon palm sugar
1 teaspoon tamarind paste

You will also need a spiralizer (see page 13)

Put the chicken in a large bowl, add the curry powder and salt, and massage the spices and salt into the chicken thighs until they are coated all over. Set aside.

While those flavors are doing their job, use a spiralizer to turn your sweet potato, daikon radish, and zucchini into noodles. Put them in a large mixing bowl.

Make the dressing by placing the chilies, lime juice, fish sauce, palm sugar, and tamarind paste into a blender and blending well. Pour the dressing on top of the vegetable noodles and mix thoroughly, then place in the fridge until you are ready to serve.

Now make the satay sauce. Heat the oil in a frying pan over medium heat, add the curry paste, and fry for 2 minutes, or until aromatic. Pour in the coconut milk and chicken stock and then add the peanut butter, sugar, fish sauce, tamarind paste, lime leaves, and lime juice. Bring to a boil, then reduce the heat and simmer for about 5 minutes, or until it has reduced and become a richly flavored satay sauce.

Get a frying pan hot and add the oil. Fry the chicken, skin-side down, for 4–5 minutes, or until golden and crispy. Turn over and cook for another 4–5 minutes, or until the chicken is cooked through. Remove from the pan and leave to rest for a few minutes.

Add the mint, cilantro, and basil leaves to the noodles and toss together. Transfer the noodle salad to a serving dish. Carve the chicken into slices and place on top. Drizzle with the satay sauce, garnish with the Crispy Shallots, and serve with lime halves to squeeze over, if you like.

CRISPY SHALLOTS

SERVES 8
....

¼ cup (60ml) coconut or
  canola oil
4 banana shallots, thinly
  sliced into rings

Heat the oil in a frying pan over low heat and fry the shallots for 10–15 minutes, or until they start to crisp up and turn a light golden color. Scoop out the shallots and drain on some paper towels.

For the satay sauce

1 tablespoon coconut or
  canola oil
2 heaped tablespoons Thai
  yellow curry paste
scant 1 cup (200ml) coconut
  milk
scant 1 cup (200ml) fresh White
  Chicken Stock (see page 212)
¼ cup (60g) crunchy peanut
  butter
2 tablespoons palm or brown
  sugar
1 tablespoon fish sauce
1 teaspoon tamarind paste
4 lime leaves
juice of 1 lime

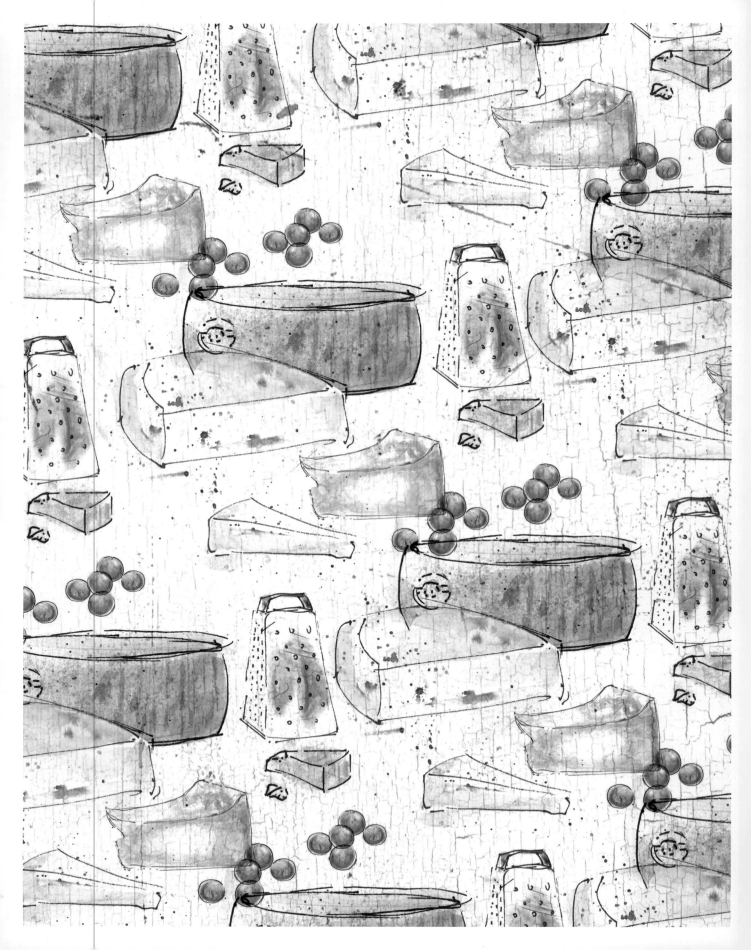

OOZE

RICH & CREAMY

BAKED OATMEAL

SERVES 6
··············

PREPARATION TIME
10 minutes

COOKING TIME
50 minutes

This baked oatmeal has the same emotional connection for me as a baked rice pudding. It is more of a brunch dish than a breakfast one. I say it's a brunch dish because it's slow-cooked in the oven, ideal for when you can't be bothered to sit and watch and stir oatmeal. It takes almost an hour to cook from start to finish, but it's worth it. In Scotland, we would have eaten this pretty plain, made with milk and a touch of salt, then scooped out of the dish and topped with brown sugar and more milk, but here I've made a healthier version that omits the sugar and will put lots of goodness into your body. I make this looser than most baked oatmeal, since I hate heavy oatmeal.

Preheat your oven tc 400°F (200°C) and liberally grease a baking dish with coconut oil.

Put the oats and oat bran in a large mixing bowl. In a separate bowl or large jug, combine the mashed bananas, milk, vanilla extract, sugar or syrup, and salt and stir. Pour this mixture over the oats and leave to stand for 5 minutes, or until the oats start to absorb the liquid.

Arrange the blueberries and raspberries in the prepared baking dish, pour the oat mixture over the top, and bake for 25 minutes. Sprinkle the flaked almonds on top, then return to the oven and continue to bake for another 25 minutes, or until golden brown on top. Allow to cool for 5 minutes, then serve with more almond milk if required.

coconut oil, for greasing
2¼ cups (200g) rolled oats
3 tablespoons oat bran
2 bananas, mashed
4¼ cups (1 liter) milk or almond
  milk
1 teaspoon vanilla extract
2 tablespoons coconut sugar
  or maple syrup
½ teaspoon salt
3½ oz (100g) blueberries
  (about ½ cup)
3½ oz (100g) raspberries
  (about ¾ cup)
toasted flaked almonds,
  to garnish

MAKES 7 PORTIONS (enough
for 1 person for a week)
....
PREPARATION TIME
5 minutes
COOKING TIME 15 minutes

POWER PORRIDGE

Oatmeal is probably the ultimate power food, but it's full of carbohydrates so I wanted to create a lower-carb porridge that still packed a good fiber punch. I've used classic rolled oats as the base (I prefer rolled oats for texture but you can use pinhead oats if you prefer), then added in oat bran for more fiber, and pimped-up the protein factor with quinoa, amaranth flakes, and some chia seeds. This is really delicious and takes away the heaviness you sometimes get when you just eat oats.

....

Place the oats, oat bran, quinoa and amaranth flakes, and chia seeds in a bowl and mix well, then transfer to a food storage container. Alternatively, you can put the ingredients directly into the container, put the lid on, and shake it like crazy until you're sure it's all mixed up. This oat mixture will last for ages in a sealed container. I tend to make a batch of this on a Sunday night to get me through the week.

To make the porridge, place 2 tablespoons of the oat mixture in a saucepan and cover with the milk. You can add a pinch of salt at this stage if you like. I really think it needs some salt but some people are funny about that kind of thing so I leave it up to you. Now cook the porridge over low heat. I like to do this really slowly for about 10–15 minutes. Sometimes it feels like the mixture's not going to absorb all the milk but it does. When it's ready it looks like (I'm sorry for this reference) wallpaper paste: porridge should be a pouring consistency not a dropping-off the spoon one. Spoon the porridge into a bowl, pour in the syrup, and then add the toppings.

For mango, passion fruit, and coconut porridge, make the porridge as above, but replace the milk or almond milk with coconut milk or, for a skinnier version, half coconut milk and half coconut water. Top the porridge with the mango, passion fruit seeds, and toasted coconut.

generous ½ cup (100g) rolled
  oats
2 tablespoons oat bran
2 tablespoons quinoa flakes
2 tablespoons amaranth flakes
2 tablespoons chia seeds

Per portion
1¼ cups (300ml) milk or almond
  milk
a pinch of salt (optional)
½–1 tablespoon maple syrup or
  coconut palm nectar

*Peach & berry topping
  (per portion)*
½ peach, chopped
about ¼ cup (50g) mixed berries
1 tablespoon milled seeds and
  flaxseeds

*Mango, passion fruit & coconut
porridge (per portion)*
1¼ cups (300ml) coconut milk (or
  half coconut milk and half
  coconut water)
½ ripe but firm mango,
  chopped
seeds of ½ passion fruit
1 tablespoon toasted shredded
  coconut

PREPARATION TIME
15 minutes

COOKING TIME
20 minutes

MOZZARELLA EN CAROZZA

I can tell you exactly where I was the first time that I had mozzarella en carozza. It was at a family-run restaurant off the Kings Road called La Famiglia. We used to go there pretty much just for the mozzarella en carozza and their lamb chops. It was my sister Cora's favorite. This dish comes in a few guises, mostly floured, egged, and then breadcrumbed and served with a tomato and basil or tomato and anchovy sauce, but I like it the way we always used to get it, which was kind of like a french toast fried cheese sandwich. So that's how I've done it here.

To make the tomato sauce, heat the oil in a small saucepan, add the garlic and basil, and fry gently for 1–2 minutes, or until aromatic and softened but not too golden. Pour in the passata, add the vinegar and sugar, and cook slowly for about 15 minutes, or until thickened. A good indicator as to whether the sauce is done is when the oil starts to split a little. Season with salt and pepper and whiz in a blender or with an immersion blender to make a smooth sauce. Keep warm.

To make the mozzarella en carozza, cut the crusts off the bread and slice the ball of mozzarella into 4. Using a rolling pin, roll out each slice of bread like pastry until it's really thin. Brush one side of each piece of bread with the egg and then lay a slice of mozzarella in the center of 4 of the slices. Use the other 4 slices of bread (egged-side down) to cover the mozzarella and make 4 sandwiches. With a 4in (10cm) round pastry cutter, cut out the mozzarella sandwich like ravioli. Squeeze the edges of the bread together to seal the edges.

Heat the oil in a large frying pan. Add the butter and, once it's melted and foaming, lay each of the mozzarella sandwiches in the hot butter. Fry for 1 minute and then turn over and fry for a further minute on the other side. Repeat this until the sandwiches are crisp and golden on each side. Remove from the pan with a spatula and drain both sides on paper towel, then sprinkle with sea salt.

Divide the sauce between plates, lay a mozzarella en carozza on top, and serve piping hot with basil leaves to garnish.

For the tomato sauce

3 tablespoons olive oil
3 garlic cloves, very finely chopped
1 basil sprig, plus a few extra leaves to garnish
1⅔ cups (400ml) tomato passata or purée (I make my own by blending a 14oz/400g can of cherry tomatoes)
splash of sherry or red wine vinegar
pinch of sugar
sea salt flakes and freshly ground black pepper

For the mozzarella en carozza

8 slices of white bread
1 x 4½ oz (125g) ball of mozzarella cheese
2 free-range eggs, beaten
2 tablespoons olive oil
1 tablespoon butter

SERVES 4
....

PREPARATION TIME
10 minutes, plus cooling

COOKING TIME
15 minutes

EGG & ONIONS
TO SANDWICH OR NOT TO SANDWICH?

Essentially this recipe is just the best egg salad filling for a sandwich. Egg and onions are a massive deal in Jewish food, so much so that I had to ask about 20 people how they made theirs and received such different results. Some people made a classic egg salad and stuffed it with sliced scallions; some cooked down their onions in schmaltz; others simply used chopped and salted raw white onions. My version is a mixture of all: I slowly cook white onions in salted schmaltz, then whip them into an egg salad and finish with plenty of very thinly sliced scallions. The person who gave me the biggest insight into the perfect egg and onions was my friend Elly Curshen who runs the Pear Café in Bristol. She makes a sandwich in honor of her Grandma Angela that she sells at the café. Her egg and onions are served in challah bread with pickles and Little Gem lettuce leaves. I've gone a step further by using gribenes as well, but you can play with the recipe to make it your own.

....

Bring a saucepan of water to a boil. Boil the eggs for 9 minutes, and then transfer them to a bowl of ice water and leave to cool.

Heat the schmaltz in a small frying pan over low heat. Add the onions and a good pinch of salt and fry for 10–15 minutes, or until the onions have softened but don't have any color. Leave to cool for 15 minutes.

Once the eggs are cold, peel and grate them on the coarse side of a grater, then put them in a large mixing bowl. Add the mayonnaise, fried onions, and scallions, mix together, and season with plenty of salt and pepper.

Serve the egg mixture on a tray with the gribenes on top and the challah bread on the side or make into open sandwiches topped with whichever of the serving ideas you feel like.

Makes 4 sandwiches

8 free-range eggs (I like to use pasture-raised eggs)
2 tablespoons Schmaltz (see page 216)
2 onions, finely chopped
5 tablespoons mayonnaise
3 scallions (white and green parts), finely sliced
sea salt flakes and freshly ground black pepper

To serve

3½oz (100g) Gribenes (see page 216)
8 slices of challah bread

And if you fancy pimping it

4 dill pickles, thinly sliced
a few dill fronds
1 Little Gem lettuce (optional)

PREPARATION TIME
30 minutes, plus cooling

COOKING TIME
10 minutes

AVOCADO SHRIMP WITH KOREAN ROASTED SHRIMP OIL MARIE ROSE SAUCE

Making a rich, roasted shrimp oil for the base of your mayonnaise gives the sauce a really intense bisque flavor. Otherwise it's just a classic Marie Rose—except it's not because instead of Tabasco sauce I've used Sriracha chili sauce and instead of cayenne pepper I've used Korean chili powder, which gives it an Asian tang that I think improves the flavor.

....

First you need to make your roasted shrimp oil. Peel the shrimp, keeping the shells to one side and the shrimp to the other. Heat the vegetable oil in a saucepan over medium heat, then add the shrimp shells and start to fry them. To begin with, a lot of liquid will come out of the shells but this will evaporate and then the shrimp shells will begin to fry. Fry for 3–4 minutes, bashing the heads to get all the juice out, until the shells turn lightly golden. Leave to infuse for 20 minutes, then strain through a fine sieve. Discard the shells and leave the roasted shrimp oil to cool until it reaches room temperature.

To make the Marie Rose sauce, place the egg yolks, mustard, vinegar, and some salt and pepper in a mixing bowl. Combine the roasted shrimp oil with the olive oil in a jug. With an electric hand mixer, beat the egg mixture and very slowly trickle the combined oils into the bowl. It will take a few seconds before the mayonnaise starts to emulsify. Keep trickling in the oil until half of it has been used up, by which stage the mayonnaise should be stable and you can speed up the pour until all the oil is combined and you have a thick, wobbly mayonnaise. Season with the lemon juice and some salt and pepper. Add the ketchup, tomato paste, brandy, and Sriracha to the mayonnaise and mix together to make the sauce. It will now be a thick but coatable consistency.

Divide the lettuce between 4 plates and squeeze on some lemon juice. Place half a pitted avocado on the lettuce, squeeze on some more lemon juice, and sprinkle with a tiny bit of salt. Divide the shrimp between the avocados, then spoon on 1–2 tablespoons of the Marie Rose sauce. Sprinkle with a touch of Korean chili powder and serve.

1lb (500g) cooked small Atlantic shrimp, shells on (these will probably have been frozen)
scant 1 cup (200ml) vegetable oil
2 Little Gem lettuces, finely shredded
a good squeeze of lemon juice
2 ripe but firm Hass avocados
1 teaspoon Korean chili powder, cayenne pepper, or regular chili powder, plus more to garnish

For the Marie Rose sauce
2 super-fresh, free-range egg yolks (I use pasture-raised, since they have bright egg yolks)
1 teaspoon Dijon mustard
1 tablespoon sherry vinegar
sea salt flakes and freshly ground black pepper
scant ½ cup (100ml) extra virgin olive oil
1 tablespoon lemon juice
2 tablespoons ketchup
1 tablespoon tomato paste
1 teaspoon brandy
2 teaspoons Sriracha chili sauce

MAKES 2 SANDWICHES
....

PREPARATION TIME
10 minutes

COOKING TIME
5–10 minutes

KIMCHEESE CUBAN SANDWICH

This recipe came about by happy accident. I want to say that I created the Kimcheese Cuban Sandwich through a meeting of minds with food writer Diana Henry on Twitter but undoubtedly it had been made before. While testing the carnitas recipe for this book, I ended up with some extra and thought I'd try my hand at a Korean-inspired Cuban sandwich, since I always have kimchi and the rest of these ingredients in my kitchen. It was a winner! The pairing of kimchi's spicy sourness with melty cheese in a panini is a thing of dreams: it takes the grilled cheese sandwich to the next level. If you've never tried this combination, do it right now as a matter of urgency. Make the carnitas. Make sure you have leftovers. Then make this sandwich. You'll thank me...

Heat a large, cast-iron grill pan or panini press. Generously butter one side of the sourdough slices or the cut sides of the rolls and toast on the grill pan over moderate heat or in the press for 1–2 minutes, or until lightly browned. Transfer to your countertop and generously brush the buttered sides with mustard. Layer the carnitas or roast pork, Swiss cheese, kimchi, scallions, and pickles on top of the mustard on 2 of the slices of bread or rolls and close the sandwiches.

Generously brush the outsides of the sandwiches with butter and set them on the grill pan or panini press; if using a pan, top the sandwiches with a baking sheet and weigh it down with something heavy, like a cast-iron skillet. Toast the sandwiches over moderate heat on the grill pan for 3 minutes per side, or toast for 3 minutes in total in a press, until the sandwiches are browned and crisp on the outside and the cheese is melted. Cut the sandwiches in half and serve piping hot and oozy. Warning: the fillings will dribble all down your face.

plenty of softened butter
2 thick slices of sourdough bread or 2 panini rolls or baby ciabatta rolls
1 tablespoon French mustard
about 10oz (300g) leftover Carnitas (see page 130) or roast pork
9oz (250g) thinly sliced Swiss cheese, such as Emmental
3½oz (100g) Gizzi's Kimchi (see page 217), roughly chopped
2 scallions, finely chopped
3 half-sour dill pickles

PREPARATION TIME
30 minutes, plus soaking,
chilling, and resting

COOKING TIME 1¾ hours

WILD MUSHROOM, TRUFFLE & TUNWORTH PIE

Let's look at what we have here: a whole Tunworth cheese (a British soft cheese from Hampshire—or you can use Camembert) set inside a layer of truffled mushrooms wrapped in puff pastry. This is what the French would call a pithivier and we would describe as a fancy turnover or pie—I'm going with pie! The whole thing is baked to a perfect golden puff, and when it's ready to eat (alongside a bitter leaf salad) it is the perfect combo of oozy, truffley goodness.

·············

2 tablespoons (30g) butter
10oz (300g) chestnut mushrooms, chopped
10oz (300g) Portobello mushrooms, chopped
1oz (25g) porcini mushrooms (rehydrated in 2 cups/500ml boiling water for 1 hour, then drained, reserving the stock)
2 garlic cloves, finely chopped
a few thyme sprigs, leaves picked
3½ tablespoons all-purpose flour, plus extra for dusting
3½ tablespoons Madeira
scant ½ cup (100ml) heavy cream
¾oz (20g) Parmesan cheese, grated
1 teaspoon sherry or tarragon vinegar
1–2 teaspoons white truffle oil
sea salt flakes and freshly ground black pepper
1 x 1lb (500g) or 2 x 14oz (400g) packages of ready-rolled all-butter puff pastry (you need two sheets)
1 x 9oz (250g) Tunworth cheese or Camembert
2 egg yolks, whisked

Melt the butter in a frying pan over high heat and fry the chestnut and Portobello mushrooms, in batches if necessary, until they have browned and are softened. Return all the fried mushrooms to the pan, add the porcini mushrooms, and fry for a further couple of minutes. Now add the garlic and thyme and cook for another minute or two. Whisk in the flour and let it cook for 1 minute, then whisk in the Madeira and the reserved porcini mushroom stock, bring to a boil, and cook until the mixture has thickened to a coating consistency. Stir in the cream, Parmesan, vinegar, and truffle oil and season with salt and pepper. Leave to cool, then transfer to the fridge until cold. The mushroom filling needs to be cold or the pastry will get warm and be ruined.

Unroll the pastry sheets and place them on separate baking trays lined with parchment paper. Roll each sheet out into a large square that will enable you to cut out 2 circles of pastry: one 12in (30cm) and one 14in (35cm) in diameter. Discard the trimmings.

Spoon one-third of the cold mushroom mixture on to the smaller pastry circle. Place the Tunworth or Camembert on top and then cover with the remaining mushroom mixture. Brush egg wash around the outer edge of the pastry. Cover with the larger pastry circle and press lightly to remove any trapped air. Select a bowl that is slightly larger than the dome of the pie and invert it over the pastry. Press down on the bowl to seal the pie edges. With a small sharp knife, scallop the edges and discard the trimmings. Brush the top of the pie with egg wash. With a paring knife, cut a pinwheel pattern in the top of the pie, stopping short of the scalloped edge. Chill in the fridge for 30 minutes.

Preheat the oven to 375°F (190°C).

Bake the pie for 30 minutes, or until it's golden and the pastry has puffed up. I suggest you leave it to rest for 30 minutes before eating, otherwise the cheese will ooze all over the place.

BRAISED VEAL TAIL WITH SAFFRON RISOTTO & BONE MARROW GREMOLATA

This recipe is based on osso bucco, but instead I've used veal tail. The meat becomes gelatinous from being cooked with marrowbone, and you get to eat the marrow at the end in a marrow gremolata, which enriches the dish, making the whole sticky process even more rich. The saffron risotto is elegant and lifting with an acidulated tang that balances the whole thing out. It's a labor of love in both the sourcing of ingredients and the making, and it's not for the faint-hearted, since it's richer than rich. I dread to think what the calorie count would be, but it has to be one of the most delicious and satisfying things you can eat. If you want to make life a little bit easier for yourself, you can cook the stew the day before, which will allow all the flavors to emulsify.

¼ cup (60ml) olive oil, plus extra to rub over the marrow bones
1 tablespoon (15g) butter
2 veal tails, cut into segments and trimmed of most of the excess fat
sea salt flakes and freshly ground black pepper
2 onions, finely chopped
2 carrots, finely chopped
2 celery sticks, finely chopped
1 teaspoon tomato paste
1 teaspoon all-purpose flour
1 bottle of decent white wine
1½ cups (350ml) tomato passata or purée
2½-4 cups (600ml–1 liter) fresh Veal or Beef stock (see page 213)
1 bay leaf
a few parsley sprigs
a few thyme sprigs
a few rosemary sprigs
a few celery leaves
4 veal marrow bones, each about 2¼in (6cm) long

Preheat the oven to 300°F (150°C).

Heat 2 tablespoons of the oil and the butter in a frying pan. Season the veal tails with plenty of salt and pepper, then add them to the frying pan and brown the meat on all sides, paying particular attention to rendering the fat down. Remove from the pan and set aside.

In a Dutch oven that's large enough to hold all the veal, heat the remaining 2 tablespoons of oil. Add the onions, carrots, and celery (this mix is called a soffrito in Italian cooking) and cook slowly for 10–15 minutes, or until sweet and softened but not really taking on much color. Add the tomato paste and ramp up the heat. Fry the vegetables and the paste for 2–3 minutes, or until a little caramelized. Add the flour and cook for 1 minute. Slowly add in the wine, then add the tomato passata or purée and stock. Add the veal tails to the sauce, along with all the herbs and plenty of freshly ground black pepper. Lay a sheet of damp parchment paper over the top of the stew and place the lid firmly on top of the pot.

Put this in the oven and slowly braise for 4½ hours, or until the meat is falling off the bone. Carefully remove the veal tails from the pot, wiping away any of the soffrito, and set aside. Strain the sauce through a fine sieve into a saucepan and discard the vegetables and herbs. You should have about 4 cups (1 liter) of liquid left. Cook the sauce to reduce it by ≫

For the acidulated butter

1 shallot, finely sliced
⅓ cup (75ml) dry white wine
⅓ cup (75ml) white wine vinegar
3½ tablespoons (50g) butter

For the risotto

1 tablespoon olive oil
2 shallots, finely sliced
1 cup plus 3 tablespoons (250g)
   risotto rice (I use Carnaroli
   or Arborio)
scant 1 cup (200ml) dry white
   wine
2½ cups (600ml) hot fresh White
   Chicken Stock (see page 212)
   infused with a generous pinch
   of saffron threads
1½oz (40g) Parmesan cheese,
   grated, plus extra to serve
⅓ cup (90g) mascarpone cheese

For the bone marrow gremolata

small bunch of flat leaf
   parsley, finely chopped
zest of 1 lemon
1 garlic clove, finely grated
marrow from 2 of the roasted
   marrow bones
2 tablespoons of the fat from
   the roasted marrow bones
1 tablespoon extra virgin olive
   oil

« about one-third, or until the sauce becomes light, syrupy, and glossy. Return the veal to the pan and heat through.

Meanwhile, after you have removed the stew from the oven, increase the oven temperature to 425°F (220°C). Rub the marrow bones with oil and season liberally with salt and pepper. Roast the bones for 45 minutes, or until golden brown and the marrow has begun to melt.

To make the acidulated butter, put the shallot, wine, and vinegar in a saucepan and reduce until there is only about 1–2 tablespoons of liquid left. Strain the reduction through a sieve into a bowl, then use a small immersion blender or whisk to beat the reduction together with the butter. Chill the acidulated butter in the fridge. You will use this as the base for the risotto.

To make the risotto, heat the oil and half of the acidulated butter in a large sauté pan. Add the shallots and fry for 5–8 minutes, or until softened. Add the rest of the acidulated butter, then add the rice and fry it in the shallot-and-butter base for 1–2 minutes. Turn down the heat to medium, then pour in the wine and stir the risotto continuously until the wine has been absorbed and the rice has started to become creamy. Now, ladleful by ladleful, add the stock, stirring slowly but continuously until each ladleful has been absorbed. If you have cooked the risotto correctly, you will have used up the exact amount of stock but if you've cooked it too fast then you may need to add a splash more water. Turn off the heat, top with the Parmesan and mascarpone, and rest the rice, covered, for 5 minutes. Remove the lid and stir.

While the risotto is resting, quickly make the gremolata by mixing all the ingredients together in a bowl.

Serve the risotto with a couple of scoops of bone marrow, a couple of pieces of the veal tail, some of the bone marrow gremolata poured over the top, and some extra grated Parmesan.

ROASTED BABY CAULIFLOWERS WITH CHEESE SAUCE

This is traditional English cauliflower cheese made even better. Roasting the cauliflowers means you don't get that soggy, smelly old-style version; instead, the cauliflowers are sweeter, with a caramelized taste. The perfect cheese sauce and crispy shallots give this dish a more umami flavor and a delicious, sweet-textured crunch. This dish is IDEAL on its own with a salad, but I like to serve it alongside roast beef, Yorkshire pudding, horseradish sauce, and bone marrow gravy.

•••

Preheat the oven to 475°F (240°C).

Melt the butter in a frying pan. Place the baby cauliflowers in a medium-sized, ovenproof dish. Rub each cauliflower with some of the melted butter, just as you would a roast chicken, and season with salt and pepper. Roast for 20 minutes, or until golden.

Meanwhile, make the cheese sauce. Melt the butter in a saucepan over medium heat. Add the flour and cook for a few minutes, stirring to form a roux. Gradually whisk in the milk, a little at a time. Add the bay leaf, mustard, and spices and cook for 10–15 minutes, or until you have a thickened and smooth sauce. Remove the sauce from the heat, add the cheeses, and stir until the cheese is well combined and melted.

Pour the cheese sauce over the roasted cauliflowers and return to the oven to bake for a further 15 minutes, or until golden.

Sprinkle the Crispy Shallots over the cauliflower cheese and serve straightaway.

3½ tablespoons (50g) butter
8 baby cauliflowers
sea salt flakes and freshly ground black pepper
Crispy Shallots (see page 79)

For the cheese sauce

3 tablespoons (40g) butter
¼ cup (40g) all-purpose flour
2½ cups (600ml) milk
1 bay leaf
1 rounded teaspoon English mustard
grating of nutmeg
a pinch of allspice
a pinch of cayenne pepper
3oz (80g) Cheddar cheese, grated
3oz (80g) Parmesan cheese, grated

CHAR

MEATY & GRILLED

GRILLED CAULIFLOWER WITH CURRIED HUMMUS & CASHEW BRITTLE

My friend Ben Denner, who runs the burger restaurant Lucky Chip and grill restaurant Licky Chops, blew my mind one day with the simplest barbecued head of broccoli with yogurt and mustard seeds. It was a testament to great ingredients being cooked simply and showed that brassicas take well to a barbecue or grill pan. So I went away and experimented with some cauliflower and came up with this show-stopper.

··

Bring a medium saucepan of salted water to a boil. Add the cauliflower and poach for 3–4 minutes, or until cooked but still pretty al dente. Drain and then transfer to a bowl of iced water to cool down quickly. Leave for 2 minutes, then drain again and pat dry with paper towel.

To make the curry oil, heat the oil in a small saucepan, add the curry leaves, and fry for about 2 minutes. Add the curry powder, turn off the heat, and leave to infuse until the oil is cold. Strain the oil into a jug and discard the leaves.

To make the cashew nut brittle, make a dry caramel by melting the sugar in a small frying pan over lowish heat until it becomes a rich golden mahogany color. Add the cashews and stir quickly, then pour onto parchment paper and leave to cool. When completely cool, use a knife to chop the brittle into ¼in (5mm) pieces or pulse quickly in a food processor to break up.

To make the curried hummus, pour one-third of the curry oil into a bowl with the curry powder and hummus and mix.

To make the dressing, pour one-third of the curry oil into a bowl with the cilantro, chili, and lemon juice, season with salt, and mix well.

Light a barbecue or heat a grill pan until searingly hot. Cut the cauliflower into quarters through the root and rub the remaining curry oil over the cauliflower. Grill it until golden and charred on all sides.

Divide the hummus between 4 plates and smooth out. Top the hummus with a wedge of cauliflower, drizzle with a little of the dressing, sprinkle with some of the cashew nut brittle and Crispy Shallots, and serve.

1 cauliflower, leaves removed and carved into a stalk
Crispy Shallots (see page 79)

For the curry oil

⅔ cup (150ml) vegetable oil
handful of curry leaves
1 teaspoon curry powder

For the cashew brittle

½ cup (100g) organic cane sugar
3½oz (100g) cashews, roasted

For the curried hummus

1 teaspoon curry powder
1 x 10oz (300g) tub of hummus

For the dressing

½ small bunch of cilantro leaves, finely chopped
1 small red chili, finely chopped
squeeze of lemon juice
sea salt flakes

PREPARATION TIME
10 minutes, plus cooling

COOKING TIME
10 minutes

GRILLED BROCCOLI WITH BURRATA, CHILI & ALMONDS

One of the first things that I ever cooked without my mother was a recipe from my colleague Dave when I worked at Cold Steel piercing studio. It was broccoli with a dressing of toasted almonds, lemon, and good olive oil and it was delicious. The recipe has since evolved and I fry some garlic, chili, and anchovies in the oil. Burrata, if you've not had it before, is similar to mozzarella cheese but enriched in the center with MORE CREAM—one of the wonders of the food world.

Bring a large saucepan of salted water to a boil. Put the whole piece of broccoli in the pan and boil for 3 minutes, or until the stem is al dente. Drain, then plunge the broccoli into a bowl of iced water. This will stop it cooking and help it to keep its vibrant green color. As soon as it's cool, carefully remove from the bowl and drain on paper towel.

Heat a grill pan over high heat (a barbecue would work brilliantly for this, too). Using a pastry brush, lightly brush the broccoli with a tablespoon of the oil and season with salt and pepper. Griddle the broccoli for 3–4 minutes, or until charred on each side. The char really adds to the flavor so don't be shy about it, though you don't want to completely blacken it. Remove from the pan and leave to cool for 20 minutes.

Meanwhile, you can toast your almonds and make the dressing. Heat 1 tablespoon of oil in a frying pan over medium heat and add the almonds. Toast them for 1 minute, or until they are pale golden, then remove with a slotted spoon and set aside. Add the garlic and chili to the frying pan and very slowly fry them for about 1–2 minutes to soften. Add the anchovies and melt them into the oil, then remove from the heat and pour in the lemon juice. Pour the dressing into a bowl and season with plenty of salt and pepper. Leave to cool for 20 minutes.

Break up the burrata and lay it out over the base of a platter. Drizzle with the remaining oil and sprinkle with sea salt. Place the whole half of the broccoli, cut-side up, on top and drizzle with a good couple of tablespoons of the dressing. Finally, sprinkle with the toasted almonds and serve.

½ head of broccoli
3 tablespoons olive oil
3 tablespoons marcona almonds, peeled
2 garlic cloves, finely chopped
1 red chili, thinly sliced
3–4 salted anchovies in olive oil
1 tablespoon lemon juice
1 x 5oz (150g) burrata cheese, removed from the fridge a good 30–60 minutes before using
sea salt flakes and freshly ground black pepper

PREPARATION TIME
30 minutes, plus curing
(preferably overnight)

COOKING TIME 3½ hours

PORK BELLY BO SSAM WITH SOUPED-UP SSAM JAM

This is the dish that made me fall head-over-heels for Korean food, not in Korea but in New York. I went there to brush up on the best ways to cook and eat Korean bo ssam, and the best and most original was David Chang's recipe—it had a hint of authenticity, but also some improvements like a pimped-up ssam jam sauce. I've taken his recipe and adapted it by using a smaller and easier-to-work-with cut of meat (pork belly) and then cooking the ssam jam sauce in the pork juices and sticky porkiness that you get at the bottom of the roasting pan. This is a brilliant way to cook meat and serve a roast in a lighter way.

We are going to start by curing the meat. This will take out all the excess moisture, season the pork belly, and give perfect flavor to the meat. To begin with, mix together the sugar and salt in a bowl and then rub the mixture all over the meat EXCEPT for the skin. Then season the pork skin with salt—the salt will allow the skin to crisp up but sugar would stop that. Cover the pork belly with plastic wrap and place in the fridge to cure for a minimum of 3 hours but ideally overnight.

Heat your oven to as hot as it will go. For most people, that's 450°–475°F (230–240°C). Place the pork in a roasting pan and roast for 20 minutes. Lower the oven temperature to 300°F (150°C) and roast the pork for 3 hours, or until you can put a fork into the meat and twist it and the flesh pulls apart. Leave to rest for 10 minutes.

While the pork is cooking you can get on with preparing the accompaniments. Start with the ssam jam sauce. Simply mix everything together in a bowl and set aside.

Place the kimchi in a food processor and process to a purée. Transfer this to a small serving or dipping bowl.

Once the meat has rested for 10 minutes, transfer the pork to a wooden board while you finish making the ssam jam sauce. Pour out any excess oil from the roasting pan. At the bottom of the pan there will be loads of sticky porky gunge. Pour the prepared ssam jam mixture into the pan, place it on the stovetop, and cook over low heat, stirring and scraping away at the bottom of the tray to pick up all the porkiness, until the sauce has reduced a little. Pour the sauce into a small serving or dipping bowl.

6 tablespoons brown sugar
6 tablespoons table salt, plus
  extra to season the pork skin
4½–5½lb (2–2.5kg) pork belly
5oz (150g) Gizzi's Kimchi
  (see page 217)

*For the souped-up ssam jam
  sauce*

3 tablespoons toasted sesame
  oil
4 tablespoons ssamjang
  (fermented soybean-and-
  chili paste)
3 tablespoons rice vinegar
1 tablespoon sugar

To serve

Romaine lettuce
cooked sushi rice (about ⅓ cup/
  60g per person)
Sesame Scallions (see opposite)

Now you're ready to serve the pork with all the components—the Romaine lettuce leaves, dips, and rice. Remove the crackling at the table and use 2 forks to shred the meat. Roll up portions of the pork in the lettuce leaves along with a bit of rice (or you could serve the rice on the side in bowls) and top with the Kimchi, Sesame Scallions, and ssam jam sauce.

SESAME SCALLIONS

5 scallions (green parts only), very thinly sliced into rings
1–2 hot green chilies, thinly sliced
2 tablespoons toasted sesame oil
¼ teaspoon salt
¼ teaspoon white pepper
½ teaspoon sugar

Simply mix together the scallions, chilies, sesame oil, salt, white pepper, and sugar together in a bowl.

SERVES 6
....

PREPARATION TIME
30 minutes, plus marinating
overnight

COOKING TIME 25 minutes

LAMB "SHAWARMA" WITH BURNED PITA, HUMMUS & POMEGRANATE TABBOULEH

1 leg of lamb, deboned (you can
    ask your butcher to do this)
2 x 10oz (300g) tubs of hummus
olive oil, for drizzling
1¾oz (50g) pine nuts, toasted
6-8 white, brown, or granary
    pita breads, charred,
    to serve

For the marinade

⅓ cup (75ml) olive oil
6 rosemary sprigs, leaves
    picked
8 thyme sprigs, leaves picked
a small bunch of mint, leaves
    picked
a small bunch of flat leaf
    parsley, leaves picked
1 bulb of garlic, cloves peeled
1 tablespoon ground cumin
2 teaspoons ground coriander
2 teaspoons paprika
1 teaspoon ground cinnamon
zest of 1 lemon

For the pomegranate tabbouleh

1¾ cups (250g) medium bulgar
2 tablespoons lemon juice
2 tablespoons pomegranate
    molasses
¼ cup (60ml) olive oil
sea salt flakes and freshly
    ground black pepper
seeds from 1 pomegranate
a small package (about 1oz/30g)
    of flat leaf parsley, leaves
    picked and roughly chopped
a small package (about 1oz/30g)
    of mint, leaves picked and
    roughly chopped

Strictly speaking, shawarma lamb is the Lebanese version of a gyro, which is made by piling up marinated meat on a giant skewer, the outside is grilled and then carved—which is kind of hard to do at home. I have taken the spices, pimped them up, and put them into a marinade for a boneless leg of lamb that is then barbecued medium-rare and served Beiruti-style (on top of hummus), alongside a piquant and punchy pomegranate tabbouleh. This is a terrific, quick, and bountifully delicious way to serve roast lamb.

....

To make the marinade, place the oil, rosemary, thyme, mint, parsley, garlic, spices, and lemon zest in a food processor and process until smooth.

Open up the leg of lamb and rub it all over with the herby marinade. Cover with plastic wrap, place in the fridge, and leave to marinate overnight.

You can cook the leg of lamb in one of two ways: either barbecuing the whole thing from start to finish in a barbecue with a lid, or charring the lamb on a grill pan and then finishing it in the oven. So here is how you cook it using both methods:

To barbecue the lamb, place a good layer of coal, about palm-length deep, and a couple of igniters in the base of the barbecue, and add some wood chips if you fancy. Light the barbecue, making sure the vent at the bottom is just open, and leave until the coals become white-red before cooking. Move the coals to the side of the barbecue to form a semicircle around the edge. When the barbecue is ready, place the leg of lamb over the hot-coal side of the barbecue and lightly char the outside all over. When nicely browned, move the lamb over to the side with no coals and then put the lid on with the vent only just open. The temperature gauge should come up to between 350°F (180°C) and 375°F (190°C). Smoke-roast the lamb for 20 minutes, turning halfway through, for medium-rare meat. Remove from the barbecue, cover with foil, and leave to rest for 15 minutes.

To cook the lamb in a grill pan and then roast, heat the oven to 425°F (220°C). Now heat a grill pan until smoking. Brown the leg of lamb on all sides in the grill pan and then place in a roasting pan. Roast for 30–35 minutes, or until medium-rare. Remove from the oven, cover with foil, and leave to rest for 15 minutes.

Meanwhile, make the tabbouleh. Cook the bulgar in a saucepan of salted boiling water for 10 minutes, or until perfectly cooked. Drain and leave to steam with the lid on for 5 minutes. Mix together the lemon juice, pomegranate molasses, and oil in a bowl with lots of seasoning. While the bulgar is still warm, dress it with half this dressing, then add the pomegranate seeds and chopped herbs and leave to stand for 10 minutes so that the flavors homogenize.

When the lamb is cooked and rested, spread the hummus over a large serving platter. Carve the lamb and place on top of the hummus, then pour over any lamb juices. Drizzle with the olive oil, scatter with the pine nuts, and serve alongside the tabbouleh and charred pita.

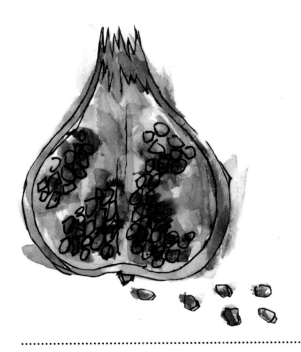

VEAL CHOPS WITH SAGE & LEMON BUTTER

Veal is the most delicate of meats in both flavor and butter-like texture. We don't really eat much of it in this country, mainly because people assume it's unethical, which is a shame. Dairy cows are bred for milk and not for their meat, so the male calves don't have any use—it's a harsh reality of the food chain. A more ethical veal is rose veal; the calf gets time to hang with its mama and roam around fields in daylight. You should check it out— it's delicious.

••

Place the butter, garlic, sage, rosemary, and lemon zest in a food processor and blitz until you have a smooth herb butter base.

Heat the oil in a frying pan and make sure the frying pan gets really hot. Season the veal chops with plenty of salt and pepper. Lay them in the hot frying pan and fry for 2 minutes on each side, or until they are a good caramelized color on both sides. Turn down the heat and turn the chops over again onto the side that was first browned. Add a couple of tablespoons of the herb butter. Let the butter melt slowly and tilt the chops to make sure the butter gets underneath them. Slowly cook the chops in the butter for another 1–2 minutes. The butter will make the chops caramelize even more and will add so much flavor to them. Turn the chops over, add 2 more tablespoons of the butter to the pan, and finish cooking for another couple of minutes. Veal should be served medium-rare: this will take a bit of time, since the chops are quite thick. A good indicator that the chops are cooked is when the meat gets a dewy layer of juice on top when you have turned it over for the final time. Remove the veal from the pan and leave to rest for 5 minutes.

Pour the Marsala wine into the frying pan, stir to deglaze the pan, and let it bubble away until it is reduced to a glossy sauce. Once the veal has rested, add any of the meat juices to the pan.

Pour the sauce over the veal and serve. Classically, you would serve this dish with spinach but I also like to throw a small baked potato alongside it.

5 tablespoons (75g) butter
1 garlic clove
15 sage leaves
1 rosemary sprig
zest of 1 lemon
1 tablespoon olive oil
2 thick veal chops, about ½lb (200g) each, trimmed
sea salt flakes and freshly ground black pepper
3½ tablespoons (50ml) Marsala wine

SERVES 2
....

PREPARATION TIME
5–10 minutes, plus marinating

COOKING TIME
10–12 minutes

GREEK SEA BREAM STUFFED WITH LEMON & HERBS WITH FENNEL SALAD

Barbecued fish might be the simplest of dishes but, my god, when it is cooked properly it is one of the nicest things to eat—especially alongside a very thinly sliced fennel salad dressed with lemon juice, good olive oil, and fennel fronds. The sea bream is best cooked over hot coals but it is also delicious when cooked in a smoking hot grill pan or under the broiler, and there really isn't any difference in timings.

....

Place half of the lemon slices and 2 bay leaves inside each fish. In a bowl, mix together the herbs with the oil. Rub the herbs and oil into the fish and leave on a plate to marinate for a couple of hours in the fridge. Mix together the fennel slices and fronds with the oil and lemon juice in a non-reactive bowl and season with salt and pepper. Leave to macerate for 20 minutes.

Meanwhile, heat your barbecue, grill pan, or broiler. Once hot enough, take the fish out of the fridge and season with plenty of salt and a touch of pepper. Cook the fish for about 5 minutes on each side, or until cooked through. Serve the fennel salad alongside the fish.

1 lemon, thinly sliced
4 bay leaves
2 sea bream (or sea bass), about 1–1¼lb (500–600g), ask your fishmonger to gut and scale the fish
a few rosemary sprigs, leaves picked and chopped
a few thyme sprigs, leaves picked and chopped
2 tablespoons olive oil
sea salt flakes and freshly ground black pepper

For the fennel salad

2 fennel bulbs, thinly sliced, fronds picked
2 teaspoons extra virgin olive oil
a squeeze of lemon juice

PREPARATION TIME
30 minutes, plus chilling

COOKING TIME
5 minutes

TUNA TATAKI WITH YUZU, GINGER & CRISPY GARLIC

Tataki is a classic Japanese dish of seared beef. The "tak" is the sound that the meat makes when you sear it. This is my version of the modern classic—made with tuna, yuzu, and crispy garlic because tuna loves these flavors. If you make this with beef, use a splash of truffle oil because beef and truffle are fab together.

Season the piece of tuna with salt and pepper, then roll it in the sesame seeds. Set aside.

Heat the oil in a frying pan over a low heat and fry the garlic until it is just starting to color. The garlic is a very important part of this dish so try not to overcook it: you want it crisp but the garlic will taste burnt if it's even just a little overcooked. Remove the garlic with a slotted spoon and leave to drain on some paper towel.

Next, fry the ginger in the same oil until is starts to go a little golden, too. Remove from the pan and set aside with the garlic.

Heat the same pan until it is smoking hot and then fry the block of tuna for 20–30 seconds on each side. You are simply sealing the fish and want it still to be raw in the center. Remove the tuna from the pan and leave to cool. Once cool, wrap the fish in plastic wrap and pop in the freezer for 2 hours or until firm but still carvable.

Make the ponzu by mixing the soy and yuzu together in a small bowl.

To serve, very thinly carve the tuna. I would use about 10 slices per portion. Arrange the tuna on a serving platter, gently overlapping the fish slices in a long row. Top each slice of fish with a slice of garlic, a few scallions slices and some of the fried ginger, then finish by topping with some sesame seeds and serve with the ponzu.

1lb (400g) tuna fillet (from the tail end for sashimi), trimmed into a block shape
sea salt flakes and freshly ground black pepper
4 tablespoons black or white sesame seeds
⅓ cup (75ml) vegetable oil
6 garlic cloves, very thinly sliced
¾in (2cm) piece of fresh ginger root, peeled and cut into very fine julienne
2 scallions (green parts only), very thinly sliced into rings
2 tablespoons toasted black and/or white sesame seeds

For the ponzu

3 tablespoons Japanese soy sauce (I love Kikkoman)
3 tablespoons yuzu juice

SERVES 4
....

PREPARATION TIME
15 minutes

COOKING TIME
5 minutes

BURRATA WITH GRILLED PEACH, MELON & PROSCIUTTO SALAD

Creamy burrata fits in pretty much any place that mozzarella goes. I've been eating the essence of this salad for as long as I can remember. It's evolved for sure, starting as just melon and prosciutto di Parma, then adding some good olive oil, then some mozzarella, then making more of a dressing with sherry vinegar, and now swapping the mozzarella for burrata and adding grilled peaches. It's a brilliant salad that gets the best out of all its ingredients and will be a hit if you need to whip up something quickly for a summer lunch or as a last-minute appetizer.

....

Heat a grill pan over a high heat. Halve the peaches, remove the pits, and then cut each half into three pieces. Rub the peaches with a little of the oil and then lay them on the griddle and cook for 2–3 minutes on each side, or until charred. Remove with a metal spatula and transfer to a plate to cool.

Drain the burrata and dry with paper towel. Tear up the burrata and spread it over the base of a large serving platter. Next, add the melon slices (I like to do this with no rhyme or reason to it: the more rustic the better). Add the ham slices to the platter, swirled into rosettes. Then, when the peaches are cool enough to touch, add them to the salad and scatter the basil over the top. If you want to be really persnickety, you can lift up some of the burrata to overlap the melon and ham.

Now you need to make the dressing. Place the sherry vinegar in a small bowl with the remaining oil and plenty of seasoning and whisk with a sauce whisk or a fork. Pour this over the salad, finely grind on plenty more black pepper, and serve.

3 ripe but firm peaches, flat peaches, or nectarines
3 tablespoons extra virgin olive oil
2 x 7oz (200g) balls of burrata cheese
½ Cantaloupe melon, deseeded, cut into 8–10 thin slices and skin cut off
12 slices proscuitto di Parma (or Serrano ham would do nicely)
a small bunch of basil, leaves picked
1 tablespoon sherry vinegar
sea salt flakes and freshly ground black pepper

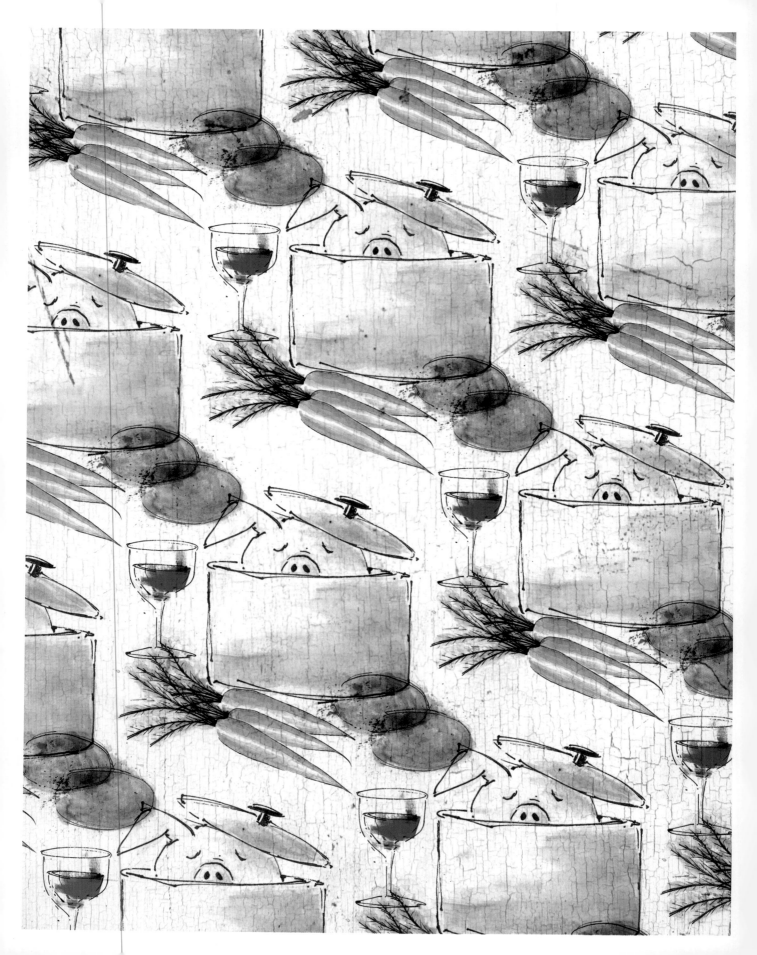

SOOTHE

SLOW-COOKED FAVORITES

PREPARATION TIME
20 minutes

COOKING TIME
1 hour

DAK DORI TANG
(KOREAN CHICKEN & POTATO STEW)

My taste buds have changed so much and I crave the heat of chilies so greatly that I'm really not sure if I would prefer a classic chicken stew to this dish. It's a simple chicken stew with English backbone but fiery Korean flavors. The gochujang (Korean chili paste) and the Korean chili powder will warm you from the inside out, and the rice wine and rice wine vinegar will add tang.

••

2 onions, 1 cut into quarters and 1 sliced into 8 wedges
6 garlic cloves
1in (3cm) piece of fresh ginger root
1 tablespoon vegetable oil
sea salt flakes and white pepper
1 whole free-range chicken, skinned and jointed into 10 pieces (you can ask your butcher to do this)
2 cups (500ml) fresh White Chicken Stock (see page 212, or water is fine)
2 rounded tablespoons gochujang (Korean chili paste)
1 tablespoon tomato paste
3 tablespoons mirin (or use sherry)
1 tablespoon rice wine vinegar
2 tablespoons soy sauce
2 teaspoons sugar
1 teaspoon Korean chili powder (use any other chili powder if you can't find it)
1lb (500g) baby potatoes, peeled
2 carrots, chopped
a bunch of scallions, each cut into 3 pieces
½lb (200g) green beans, trimmed and halved

To serve

cooked sushi rice (about ⅓ cup/ 60g per person)
scallion, very finely sliced
2 tablespoons white and/or black sesame seeds, toasted

Place the quartered onion, garlic, and ginger in a blender with a splash of water and process to a smooth paste.

Heat the oil in a large Dutch oven. Season the chicken and fry it in small batches until golden. Remove the chicken from the pot and set aside. Now fry the onion wedges for 3–4 minutes, stirring and scraping the bottom of the dish to pick up the chickeny residue, until they are tinged brown and starting to get soft, but still hold their shape. Remove the onion wedges from the pan and set aside with the chicken.

Add the onion, garlic, and ginger paste to the pot and fry for 3–4 minutes, stirring constantly, until the paste just starts to turn golden. Pour in the stock or water, then return the browned chicken and onion wedges to the dish and add the gochujang, tomato paste, mirin, rice wine vinegar, soy sauce, sugar, chili powder, potatoes, and carrots. Put the lid on and cook over medium–low heat for 35 minutes. Add the scallions and beans and cook, uncovered, for a further 5–10 minutes, or until the chicken is falling off the bone and the potatoes are cooked. If you're worried that the chicken breasts may overcook, remove them after 25 minutes and then return them to the pot to heat through at the end of the cooking time (but in Korea they wouldn't mind). Serve over sushi rice and scatter with scallions and toasted sesame seeds.

SERVES 4-6
••••••••••••••

PREPARATION TIME
30 minutes, plus soaking

COOKING TIME
2 hours

SPANISH CHICKEN STEW WITH CHORIZO, SHERRY & GARBANZO BEANS

Sherry has a bad reputation, doesn't it? It still conjures up thoughts of old ladies at Christmas but in Spain, where sherry originates, it's a whole different ball game and sherries are prized as some of the greatest wines in the world. Sherry is not only delicious to drink, it's also terrific to cook with. Together, sherry, chicken, chorizo, and garbanzo beans (wonderful Spanish chickpeas, to you and me) make this one damn sexy dish. Stews are best made the day before you need them and it's particularly worth doing so when cooking a stew with beans because it balances out the seasoning and homogenizes. A stew like this benefits from a whole chicken that's cut into pieces. It's weirdly therapeutic and much better both economically and for the environment, but if you are unable to do this you can use 8-10 pieces of chicken thighs on the bone.

••

1 cup (200g) dried garbanzo beans (chickpeas), soaked for 12 hours
2 tablespoons olive oil
1 large free-range chicken, skinned and jointed into 10 pieces (you can ask your butcher to do this)
3 whole raw cooking chorizo sausages (preferably Spanish), about ½lb (240g) in total
1 bulb of garlic, cut in half horizontally
2 onions, finely chopped
1½ cups (350ml) dry sherry
1 teaspoon sherry vinegar
4¼ cups (1 liter) fresh White Chicken Stock (see page 212)
a generous pinch of saffron
2 bay leaves
1 rosemary sprig
a few thyme sprigs, leaves picked
a small bunch of flat leaf parsley, chopped
zest of ½ lemon
sea salt flakes and freshly ground black pepper

Rinse the garbanzo beans thoroughly, place in a large pan, and cover generously with cold water. Cover with a lid and boil for 25 minutes, or until the outsides feel cooked but the centers still feel a little chalky. They will cook more in the stew.

Preheat the oven to 400°F (200°C). I like to cook my stew in stages and fry everything separately in a frying pan before building the stew in a Dutch oven but if you're worried about too much dish washing then you can, by all means, brown everything straightaway in the pot. Heat the oil in a frying pan. Season the chicken pieces with salt, then add them to the frying pan, skin-side down, in batches and brown them thoroughly. It's really worth persevering to get a good caramel color on the outside of the chicken, since this is where all the meaty flavor comes from, plus it will render down all the fat from the skin. Once the chicken pieces are browned, remove them from the frying pan with some tongs and set aside on a plate.

Brown the chorizo all over in the same frying pan, then remove and set aside. I like to cook the chorizo whole in the stew and then slice it afterwards. Next, lay the garlic bulb halves in the frying pan, cut-side down, for a minute, until golden, then remove and set aside. ≫

« Now you need to pour away the excess fat from the frying pan (there will be a fair amount) until you are left with about 2 tablespoons of oil. Add the onions and fry them slowly for about 10–12 minutes, until they have softened and have started to tinge golden, then transfer to a Dutch oven. Pour in the sherry, sherry vinegar, and stock, add the saffron, bay leaves, rosemary, thyme, and half the parsley and bring to a boil. Add the chicken, chorizo, garlic, and beans to the pot. The chicken needs to be 90 percent immersed in liquid, so top up with more stock to ensure this if necessary. Put the lid on the pot and place in the oven for 15 minutes. Turn the oven down to 350°F (180°C) and cook for a further 45 minutes.

Now, this is where it gets complicated. This isn't what most people do when cooking stews but it's what they SHOULD do. Remove the pot from the oven and carefully remove the chicken breast pieces and set aside, leaving the chorizo and chicken thighs and leg meat in the pot. There will still be a fair amount of liquid in the pot and the beans will not be fully cooked yet, so put the pot on the stovetop and cook with the lid off over lowish heat for another 15–20 minutes to reduce the sauce, making it taste nice and strong, and until the beans are cooked fully (completely tender but still holding their shape). Don't worry about the chicken thighs and leg meat—they are hard to overcook.

Once you're happy with the flavor and thickness of the stew and the beans are cooked through, return the chicken breast pieces to the pot. Remove from the heat, stir in the remaining parsley and the lemon zest, and season to taste. Put the lid on and leave the stew to rest for 10 minutes. This will make the chicken tender and the beans cooked in a uniform way.

Remove the chorizo from the pot and slice each sausage into about 10 pieces. Put the slices back in the pot and stir through. Spoon a couple of pieces of chicken, some chorizo, beans, and sauce on to each plate and serve with a fresh green salad.

BEEF CHEEK GOULASH

Beef goulash was never something that I loved or lived for. The stuff we ate when I was growing up had WAY TOO MUCH paprika for me and was thickened with rich heavy cream. The essence of my goulash is brilliant—and it's a classic. I've used beef cheek, a cut of meat that can be braised really slowly and is full of gelatine so that it cooks into a feathery, sticky, melty braised stew. I've given the goulash more body by adding ale to the braising liquid, added smokiness by using sweet smoked paprika, and finished it all off with some sour cream, which is just as it should be. Spätzle (alpine pasta) is so much fun to make and eat, and when fried in butter it is proper rib-sticking comfort food.

2 tablespoons vegetable oil
2¼lb (1kg) beef cheeks (2 cheeks), trimmed and each cheek cut in half
sea salt flakes and freshly ground black pepper
2 onions, thinly sliced
6 garlic cloves, peeled
1 tablespoon all-purpose flour
1 teaspoon hot smoked paprika
1¼ cups (300ml) light or dark ale
2 cups (500ml) fresh Beef or Dark Chicken Stock (see page 213)
2 bay leaves
1 tablespoon sweet smoked paprika
½ cup (125ml) sour cream
2 tablespoons chopped chives

For the spätzle

3 cups (400g) all-purpose flour
3½ tablespoons (50ml) milk
scant ½ cup (100ml) sparkling water
3 free-range eggs
a good pinch of nutmeg
2 tablespoons (30g) butter

Heat the oil in a large, heavy-based saucepan. Season the beef cheeks with salt and pepper, then brown all over. Remove from the pan and set aside. Add the onions and fry for 10 minutes, or until softened and golden, adding the garlic for the final minute. Then add the flour and the hot smoked paprika to the onions and stir to coat. Pour in the ale and stir until the sauce thickens, then add the stock. Return the beef cheeks to the pan with the bay leaves, stirring carefully so as not to break up the meat. Put a lid on the pan and cook on the burner's lowest setting for 3½ hours. The meat is ready when it is cooked through and melting. Add the sweet smoked paprika and season well.

To make the spätzle, mix together all the ingredients apart from the butter in a bowl. Place the batter in the fridge to rest for 10–30 minutes. Bring a large pan of salted water to a boil. Pour the batter into a colander over the pan of boiling water and use a spoon or ladle to force the batter through the holes—this will make wriggly noodles that look like tear drops. Even better, use a spätzle maker if you have one. Poach the spätzle in batches for 1–2 minutes, or until they have set, then remove with a slotted spoon and put them into a bowl of iced water.

Drain the spätzle and heat the butter in a frying pan until it is golden and nutty, then fry the spätzle noodles until they are golden. Serve the spätzle with the goulash and top with sour cream and chopped chives.

PREPARATION TIME
40 minutes

COOKING TIME
3–3¼ hours

FLAT IRON BOURGUIGNON

I love a glass of red wine, and if I have the cash I always go for a good Burgundy over anything else. It is lighter, as a whole, and simply much more refined in flavor. Boeuf Bourguignon is a simple beef and red wine stew. Purists believe that it should be made with a whole bottle of wine and no stock and that the stewing veggies should remain in the sauce. It's delicious like this but I like to refine my version by using a featherblade beef cut, which despite stewing will cook to show a bright pink middle and has a mammoth amount of tooth-sucking gelatine in it that makes for sticky, soft, falling-apart meat and a glossy sauce. I do add stock (for an even glossier and stickier sauce) and I strain out the veg, adding in the garnish afterwards for a quick cook while the sauce reduces.

olive oil
4 top blade or flat iron steaks, each about 1in (3cm) thick
sea salt flakes and freshly ground black pepper
2 carrots, roughly chopped
1 onion, roughly chopped
1 celery stick, roughly chopped, plus a handful of celery leaves
1 bulb of garlic, cut in half horizontally
1 teaspoon tomato paste
2 teaspoons all-purpose flour
2 cups (500ml) red Burgundy wine
2 cups (500ml) fresh Beef or Veal Stock (see page 213)
1 bay leaf
2 rosemary sprigs
4–5 thyme sprigs
4–5 parsley sprigs, plus 1 tablespoon chopped parsley
5oz (150g) smoked bacon lardons
12 fresh or frozen baby onions or shallots, peeled
3½oz (100g) button mushrooms
Perfect Creamy Mash (see page 128), to serve

Heat a frying pan until it is really hot. Add 1 tablespoon of oil. Season the steaks with salt and pepper and then fry them for 2–3 minutes on each side to give the beef some pretty slick caramelization. Remove from the pan and set aside.

Add a touch more oil to the pan if necessary, then add the carrots, onion, and celery and fry them over medium heat for 5–8 minutes, making sure to scrape away at the bottom of the pan with a wooden spoon to remove any meaty bits that have been left behind after frying the steaks; this will add to the flavor. For the final minute, increase the heat and make space for the garlic halves. Fry them until the cut side is golden, making sure to keep the veggies moving around the pan while the garlic is frying. Remove the garlic from the pan and set aside with the steaks.

Now add the tomato paste and fry the veggies in the paste, which will caramelize around them. Add the flour and stir to coat the vegetables. Cook the flour for 1 minute, then pour in the wine and stock and bring to a boil. Transfer to a medium Dutch oven with a lid. Lower the heat to a simmer, add the steaks, garlic, bay leaf, and the rosemary, thyme, and parsley sprigs to the pot, cover with the lid, and cook on the stovetop for 2½ hours, or until the steak is starting to fall apart.

Remove the steaks from the stew, being really careful »

« not to let them break up, and lay them on a plate. Now you need to strain out all of the stewing vegetables, so place a sieve over a large bowl and pour the liquid into the sieve. It will be fairly watery with a hint of beefy flavor. Wash out the pot and then pour the strained liquid back into it. We now want to reduce the sauce in order to make the flavor really punchy before adding in our garnishes, so put the pot back on the stovetop and bring to a gentle simmer over low heat.

Heat 1 teaspoon of oil in a large frying pan and fry the bacon lardons until the fat has rendered away and the bacon is crisp and golden. Transfer the bacon to the pot with the sauce. Add the onions to the frying pan and fry them for 3–4 minutes, stirring constantly, until they are golden, then transfer them to the pot. Finally, add a touch more oil to the frying pan and fry the mushrooms until they are golden. Transfer the mushrooms to the pot. Return the steaks to the pot and cook for about 20 minutes, or until the sauce has thickened and is really flavorful and meaty, then season to taste. Serve with Perfect Creamy Mash and chopped parsley.

PERFECT CREAMY MASH

SERVES 6
············

1¾lb (800g) potatoes, peeled
  and cut into chunks
1¼ sticks (150g) butter
3½ tablespoons (50ml) milk
2 tablespoons heavy cream
a good grating of nutmeg
tons of salt and white pepper

Boil the potatoes in a large pan of salted water for 20 minutes. Drain and leave to steam in a colander until dry, then tip out into a clean pan and mash or crush through a potato ricer until really smooth. With a balloon whisk, whip in the butter, milk, cream, and nutmeg over very low heat until it is piping hot, then season with a ton of salt and pepper before serving straight away.

PREPARATION TIME
45 minutes

COOKING TIME
4¼ hours

CARNITAS WITH GRILLED PINEAPPLE SALSA & PINK PICKLED ONIONS

Making carnitas is a bit like making a stew, although you're roasting the meat in a cast-iron pot for hours and hours with barely any liquid and relying on the natural juices of the meat and the fat to break it down. Eventually, the liquid evaporates and clings to the meat like a sticky jus and the meat then starts to fry in its own fat. It's INSANELY delicious and a fun alternative to a classic roast dinner. I've served it with a grilled pineapple salsa (making it very Mexican-Bajan), some avocado, and the obligatory pink pickled onions.

For the carnitas

2¼lb (1kg) boneless pork shoulder, fat and skin on, cut into large chunks
sea salt flakes and freshly ground black pepper
3 tablespoons cooking oil
2 cups (500ml) fresh White Chicken Stock (see page 212)
1 bulb of garlic, cut in half horizontally
2 bay leaves
2 strips of orange rind
2 cinnamon sticks
½ teaspoon coriander seeds
6 sage leaves
3 oregano sprigs

For the pineapple salsa

4 slices of fresh pineapple cut horizontally, each slice ⅓in (8mm) thick
olive oil
½ red onion, finely chopped
1 red chili, deseeded and finely chopped
2 tablespoons lime juice
a small bunch of cilantro, finely chopped

To serve

12 small corn tortillas
Pink Pickled Onions (see opposite)
1 avocado, peeled, pitted, and finely chopped, lime squeezed over, and sprinkled with salt
good Mexican hot sauce (optional)

To make the carnitas, preheat the oven to 325°F (170°C). Season the meat with salt and pepper. Heat the oil in a frying pan, then add the meat in batches and brown well, transferring each batch to a lidded cast-iron casserole or Dutch oven once browned. Pour the stock over the meat and then add the rest of the ingredients to the pot. Put the lid on and roast in the oven for 3 hours, stirring every so often. You will notice that the meat releases a fair amount of liquid. After 3 hours, remove the pot from the oven. The meat will be so soft that you are able to put a spoon through it, and that's EXACTLY what you're going to do. Remove the aromatics and then break the meat up with a spoon. Some bits will be meatier than others. Now return the pot to the oven, this time with the lid off, and bake for 15 minutes. Remove from the oven, stir to break up more of the meat, then return to the oven and repeat this every 15 minutes for 1 hour. By the end of the cooking time, the liquid will have reduced and the meat will have broken down into soft, feathery, pulled pork pieces and be frying gently in its own fat. You now have carnitas. Season with plenty of salt and pepper.

While the meat is cooking, make the accompaniments.

To make the pineapple salsa, heat a grill pan over high heat. Rub the pineapple slices with oil and grill them for 2–3 minutes on each side. Transfer to a plate and set aside until cool enough to handle, then trim off the skin and remove the core. Slice the pineapple into tiny cubes and place in a bowl. Add the onion, chili, lime juice, cilantro, and any pineapple juices that may have been released from the pineapple while it was resting.

Give it all a good mix. Leave to macerate for least 20 minutes.

Once the carnitas are cooked, heat up your tortillas in a dry frying pan. Serve all the components in seperate bowls and get your pals to help themselves. To build, lay a tortilla on a plate, top with a large spoonful of carnitas and then some pink pickled onions, pineapple salsa, and avocado. Add some Mexican hot sauce if you like it spicy.

Any leftover carnitas can be made into the Kimcheese Cuban Sandwich (see page 93).

PINK PICKLED ONIONS

SERVES 4
....

3½ tablespocns (50ml) white
  wine vinegar
2½ tablespoons sugar
1 teaspoon salt
1 red onion, thinly sliced

Place the vinegar, sugar, and salt in a saucepan and cook over low heat until they melt together. Bring to a boil for a second and then pour the liquid over the onion slices in a heatproof bowl. Cover with plastic wrap and leave to macerate for at least 2 hours at room temperature before serving.

PREPARATION TIME
30 minutes

COOKING TIME
4 hours

BOLOGNESE SAUCE – THE REAL DEAL

This is probably the only recipe that you will ever see me do that hasn't really been tweaked. This is how Bolognese should be made. It's a light sauce made with pork and veal (not beef) and has layers of earthy chicken livers and salty, smoky pancetta. It's made with WHITE wine and a slightly unusual reduction of milk, and what you get is a ragú that's as rich as it is light and tastes authentic: like one you would get in Italy or at a really good Italian restaurant. The only thing I add is garlic (apparently forbidden), and I stir through a bit of basil after a very long, slow cook. There's definitely more legwork than with your usual Bolognese sauce and it may surpass the weeknight dinner bracket but it's worth the effort and ingredients.

⅓ cup (75ml) light olive oil
just under 1lb (400g) ground
   veal (or beef)
just under 1lb (400g) ground
   pork
5oz (150g) chicken livers,
   finely chopped
sea salt flakes and freshly
   ground black pepper
5oz (150g) pancetta, thinly
   sliced and then finely
   cross-chopped
2 onions, finely chopped
2 carrots, finely chopped
2 celery sticks, finely chopped
6 garlic cloves, finely chopped
scant 1 cup (200ml) milk
1 bottle of white wine
1 x 35oz (992g) jar or can of
   plum tomatoes (I prefer
   jarred tomatoes), puréed in a
   food processor
2 tablespoons tomato paste
1–2 bay leaves
6–8 thyme sprigs
2 rosemary sprigs
a good grating of nutmeg
a few basil sprigs, stalks
   and all

Heat 2 tablespoons of oil in a large, deep Dutch oven over high heat. Season the ground meat and chicken livers and then brown the meat in batches. Remove each batch from the pot, using a slotted spoon to drain off the fat, and set aside on a plate.

Add the remaining oil to the pot, lower the heat, and fry the pancetta until the fat has rendered away and it has gone golden brown. Add the onions, carrots, and celery and cook slowly for 10 minutes, or until they have softened and started to turn golden. Add the garlic and cook for a further couple of minutes.

Return the meat to the pot, pour in the milk, and cook for about 5–10 minutes, or until the milk has reduced down. The milk adds a touch of sweetness and also softens the flavors of the acidic alcohol and tomatoes. Pour in the wine and cook for a further 5 minutes before adding the tomatoes, tomato paste, bay leaves, and the thyme and rosemary sprigs. Cook over low heat for 3 hours, or until the sauce has reduced but is still very much a pouring consistency and the meat is tender: that is the key to a proper Bolognese; it's a meat sauce.

Remove the herb sprigs from the stew and season with plenty of salt and pepper. To finish, add a grating of nutmeg and stir through the basil sprigs. I serve this with any long pasta, from pappardelle to spaghetti, and tons of freshly grated Parmesan cheese.

SERVES 6-8
....

PREPARATION TIME
15 minutes, plus making the
Bolognese Sauce

COOKING TIME 1 hour

LASAGNE

My search for the best lasagne recipe has been no mean feat. I always come back to the same philosophy: simply layering the best Bolognese sauce with sheets of fresh pasta, topping it with béchamel sauce and Parmesan cheese, and then giving it a long, slow bake. Fresh pasta, for me, is a must. It's just as easy to use as dried pasta and can be trimmed with scissors, making it easy to fit the exact size of your dish. Blanching the pasta for a few seconds prior to layering means that it doesn't soak up too much wetness from the sauce, giving the lasagne that desired (sorry for lack of better word) sloppiness.
A thick slick of béchamel sauce covered in cheese is better than layers of Bolognese and béchamel and makes the lasagne easier to cut. I love this with a crisp green salad, but there are times when I go back to my teens and serve the lasagne with fries (just don't tell anyone).

....

½ recipe quantity of Bolognese
   Sauce (see page 134)
7oz (200g) fresh lasagne
   sheets, blanched for 30
   seconds and then refreshed in
   iced water
1¾oz (50g) Parmesan cheese,
   grated

For the béchamel sauce

2 cups (500ml) milk
1 bay leaf
a really generous grating of
   nutmeg
3½ tablespoons (50g) butter
6 tablespoons all-purpose flour
1 x 9-11oz (250-300g) ball of
   mozzarella cheese (don't
   bother with buffalo
   mozzarella since it'll get
   lost in the sauce)
sea salt flakes and freshly
   ground black pepper

To make the béchamel sauce. warm the milk, bay leaf, and nutmeg together in a saucepan. Remove from the heat and leave to infuse for 10 minutes, then discard the bay leaf. Melt the butter in a saucepan, then whisk in the flour. Cook the flour for 2 minutes, and then slowly add the infused milk, whisking briskly until combined in order to make sure the sauce remains smooth. Bring the sauce to a boil slowly, making sure you keep scraping the base of the pan. Chop the mozzarella into small cubes and beat it into the sauce, allowing it to melt slowly. Season to taste with salt and pepper and more nutmeg.

Heat the oven to 350°F (180°C). Now it's time to build your lasagne. It's easier to do this when the Bolognese and béchamel sauces are both cold but if you're pushed for time it's really not a problem to do it while both sauces are hot. Lay 2-3 lasagne sheets on the base of a 16in x 10in (40cm x 20cm) baking dish. Add 2-3 ladlesful of Bolognese sauce and smooth down with the back of the ladle. Lay another layer of pasta sheets on top of the sauce and repeat twice more, finishing with a final layer of pasta. Cover the pasta with the béchamel sauce and top this with the Parmesan.

Bake the lasagne for 40 minutes, or until the sides are bubbling and the surface is golden.

....

NEW YORK-STYLE MEATBALLS & GRAVY WITH ZUCCHINI NOODLES

The first time I went to New York I wasn't an annoyingly snobby food brat like I am now. I wanted to try all the classic foods you see in the movies: eat a hot dog or a pretzel from a street cart, go to a Jewish deli, and visit Little Italy. This desire came from my love of mafia movies and *The Sopranos*, which have so many scenes showing the characters cooking a good tomato sauce—or "gravy" as it's known by Italian-Americans. In this recipe the tomato "gravy" is puréed and the meatballs are a tiny bit bigger than you might be used to. You can serve them with any long pasta but I've done them here with "zoodles" (zucchini turned into noodles with a spiralizer) that you don't need to cook because the heat of the meatballs and sauce will warm it through.

For the meatballs

2 tablespoons olive oil
3 garlic cloves, crushed
1 onion, finely chopped
1lb (450g) ground pork
1lb (450g) ground beef
a few thyme sprigs
2 rosemary sprigs
sea salt flakes and freshly
  ground black pepper

For the tomato sauce

1 tablespoon olive oil
3 onions, finely chopped
2 garlic cloves, crushed
1 tablespoon tomato paste
1 x 14oz (400g) can chopped
  tomatoes
2¼lb (1kg) fresh plum or cherry
  tomatoes, chopped
1-2 tablespoons red wine or
  sherry vinegar
1 teaspoon sugar
½ bunch of basil

To serve

1lb (400g) zucchini noodles (or
  serve with cooked pasta)
grated Parmesan cheese

You will also need a spiralizer
  (see page 13)

To make the meatballs, heat 1 tablespoon of olive oil in a saucepan, then add the garlic and onion and sweat for 4–5 minutes, or until soft and a little golden. Leave to cool. In a bowl, mix together the ground pork and beef with the sweated onion and garlic and the herbs and season well with salt and pepper. Fry a tiny bit of the meatball mixture and then taste to check the seasoning. If necessary, adjust the seasoning of the meatball mixture. Divide the mixture into 18 balls (about 3oz/80g each) and refrigerate until needed.

To make the sauce, heat the oil in a medium saucepan and sweat the onions for 10 minutes, or until soft, adding in the garlic for the last minute. Stir in the tomato paste and cook for few minutes, then add the canned tomatoes and the plum or cherry tomatoes. vinegar, and sugar. Cook the sauce slowly for about 1 hour, or until reduced but still a pouring consistency. At this stage, I like to whiz the sauce in a food processor for an Italian-American-style "gravy" but you don't have to. Return the sauce to the pan, stir through the basil, and season to taste.

While the sauce is cooking, fry the meatballs in the remaining oil in a heavy-based frying pan until they are browned and cooked through. Add the meatballs to the "gravy" and cook for a further 10 minutes.

Serve the meatballs and sauce with zucchini noodles and tons of black pepper and grated Parmesan cheese.

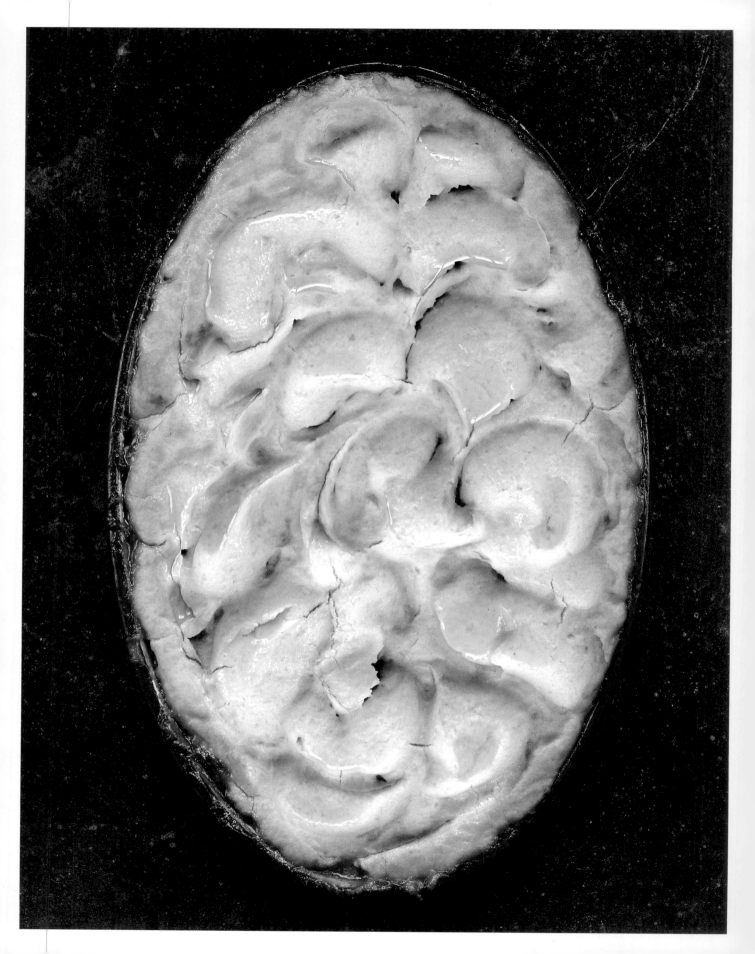

SERVES 8
....

PREPARATION TIME
40 minutes, plus cooling
(preferably overnight)

COOKING TIME 4 hours

MERGUEZ SHEPHERD'S PIE WITH CAULIFLOWER MASH

Shepherd's pie is one of my death row dinners. My mom's shepherd's pie is better than your mom's—fact! I almost didn't want to mess with the recipe but my sidekick, Sofia, uses merguez sausages to make a really great version that is spicy, rich, and sticky. The cauliflower mash is lower in carbs and is superior to mashed potatoes as a topping.

2 tablespoons olive oil, plus
   extra for drizzling
2¼lb (1kg) boneless lamb
   shoulder, cut into chunks
sea salt flakes and freshly
   ground black pepper
4 onions, finely chopped
2 carrots, roughly chopped
1 leek, roughly chopped
1 bulb of garlic, cut in half
   horizontally
1 teaspoon tomato paste
1 tablespoon all-purpose flour
1⅔ cups (400ml) white wine
4¼ cups (1 liter) fresh Dark
   Chicken or Beef Stock (see
   page 213)
1 teaspoon ras-el-hanout
   spice mix
a few thyme sprigs, leaves
   picked
3 rosemary sprigs, leaves
   picked and finely chopped
1 bay leaf
8 merguez sausages

For the cauliflower mash

1 large cauliflower, about 2lb
   (900g), broken into florets
2 tablespoons butter
3½ tablespoons (50ml) fresh
   Vegetable or Chicken Stock
   (see pages 212–13)

You need to start by braising the lamb. Heat 1 tablespoon of oil in a frying pan over lowish heat. Season the lamb well and fry it in batches until well browned on all sides, then remove the meat from the pan and set aside. Cooking the lamb in batches, leaving space around each piece of meat, means that you get much better color on the meat, rather than letting it sweat in its own juices. You won't need to add any extra oil to the pan, since the lamb has tons of fat in it. Once all the lamb has browned you should have about 2 tablespoons of fat left in the pan.

Lower the heat, add the onions, carrots, and leek and cook for 10–25 minutes, or until softened, then lay the garlic, cut-side down, in the pan for a minute until golden. Remove the garlic bulb and set aside with the lamb. Add the tomato paste to the pan with the vegetables, increase the temperature, and quickly caramelize the vegetables in the tomato paste. Add the flour and cook for a further minute. Pour in the wine and whisk together.

Transfer the meat, garlic, and vegetables to a lidded Dutch oven, add the stock, ras-el-hanout, and herbs and simmer over medium-low heat for 2 hours.

After the stew has been cooking for an hour, heat a frying pan and add the remaining oil. Squeeze the merguez sausages out of their skins and fry them on high heat until browned, as if they were ground beef. Add them to the stew and continue cooking for the remaining hour, until your stew is rich and sticky and the meat is falling to pieces. Season with salt and pepper and allow to cool. It's always best to allow a stew to chill completely to at least room temperature before trying to pile the mash on top, so I like to make mine the day before, which gives all the flavors time to harmonize together. »

«   To make the cauliflower mash, roughly chop the cauliflower in a food processor. Add the cauliflower to a large saucepan with the butter and stock, put a lid on the pan, and cook slowly or "sweat" for 8 minutes, or until the cauliflower is cooked through. Whiz in a food processor, adding a touch more stock if it needs it, until the cauliflower is smooth and resembles pomme purée.

Heat the oven to 400°F (200°C). Put the stew in a shallow oveproof dish, top the stew with the cauliflower mash, and bake for 25 minutes, or until golden and piping hot. Drizzle with olive oil and serve.

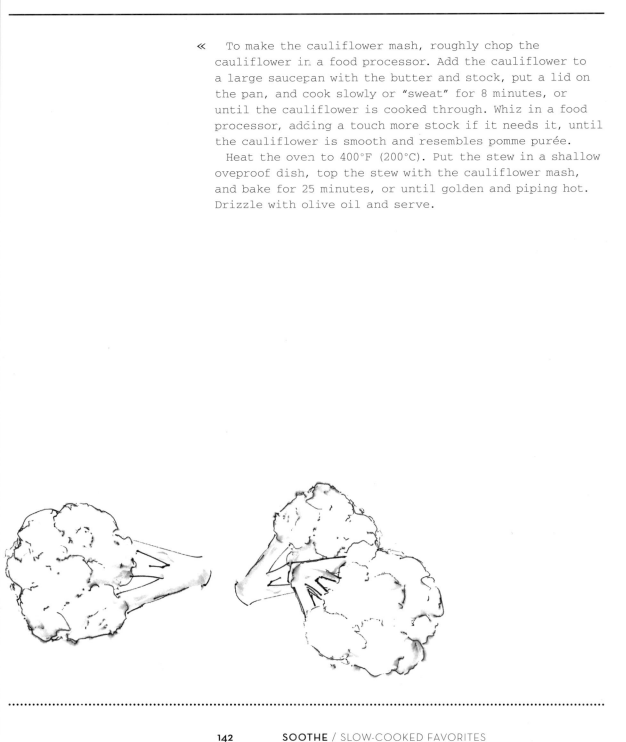

FISH STEW WITH FENNEL, SAFFRON & ORZO

The secret to a good fish stew is to use really fresh fish and really good stock. As with a good beef stew, you want your stock to leave your lips sticking together and I always make my own fish stock (see page 213). As for the fish, use what you can. I like a fish that keeps its shape, like monkfish. Everything else about this stew is simple, using flavors that marry well with the fish.

··

4¼ cups (1 liter) Fish Stock (see page 213) or good-quality shellfish stock

a generous pinch of saffron threads

2 tablespoons olive oil

1 fennel bulb, very finely chopped, fronds picked and stored in iced water

6 garlic cloves, finely chopped

½ teaspoon crushed dried chilies

1 x 14oz/400g jar or can of plum tomatoes (I like mine from a jar), processed to a purée (or you could use passata)

1 cup (250ml) dry white wine

½ cup (85g) orzo pasta

sea salt flakes and freshly ground black pepper

4 large monkfish cheeks or 1lb (500g) monkfish or any other firm fish that's good for stewing

12 raw jumbo shrimp, peeled (keep the shells for stock)

1 squid, cleaned, slashed, and cut into bite-sized pieces

2 handfuls of small clams, scrubbed clean (discard any clams that are chipped or open)

a small bunch of parsley, finely chopped

zest of 1 lemon

Before you start to cook the stew properly, heat up the stock in a saucepan until it just begins to boil. Add the saffron, reduce the heat, and simmer for 1 minute, then turn off the heat. Leave the stock to infuse with the saffron while you get on with the rest of the dish.

Heat the oil in a large Dutch oven with a lid. Add the fennel and fry gently for 5 minutes, or until softened and just starting to turn golden. Now add the garlic and chilies and continue to fry for another 2 minutes, or until the garlic and chilies are aromatic. Pour in the puréed tomatoes and slowly cook for 10 minutes, or until the tomatoes are pretty thick. Pour in the wine and cook for 1 minute, then pour in the saffron stock. Bring the stew, which will now be fairly soupy, to a slow simmer and cook for 10 minutes. You're trying to make a really intense main base flavor, so taste the stew as it's reducing and continue to reduce until you're happy with the flavor, bearing in mind that the sauce will thicken up when you put the orzo and fish into it. And that's exactly what you're going to do next, but in stages.

First add the orzo and a little salt. Orzo takes about 8–10 minutes to cook, so timing is now of the essence. After about 4 minutes you can add the firm fish to the pot. Continue to cook for 3 minutes, then add the shrimp. After another minute the squid can go in. And after about 30 seconds you can add the clams. Now cover and cook for a further 1–2 minutes, or until all the clamshells have opened (discard any that remain closed) and the fish is cooked through. Add the parsley and lemon zest and season with salt and pepper but do taste before salting, since the clams can be quite salty. Transfer the stew to a serving dish and top with the fennel fronds.

SAVOR

TASTY MAINS

GIGANTES WITH EGGS, YOGURT & HOT CHILI BUTTER

This is my version of Greek fasolia gigantes, which are tomato-braised lima beans. I use fresh tomatoes and cook the beans in two stages, first getting them almost cooked and then braising them in a tomato sauce with oregano. I serve these beans as a brunch or light supper dish with poached eggs, garlicky yogurt, fresh herbs, and hot chili butter.

••

4 free-range eggs (I use
  pasture-raised eggs, since
  they have bright egg yolks)
sea salt flakes and freshly
  ground black pepper

For the beans

1⅔ cups (300g) dried Greek
  fasolia gigantes or large
  white lima beans
scant ½ cup (100ml) olive oil
2 onions, finely chopped
1 small bulb of garlic, cloves
  peeled and finely chopped
6-7 oregano sprigs
a good pinch of dried chili
  flakes
1½lb (700g) fresh vine-ripened
  tomatoes, chopped
1 tablespoon red wine or sherry
  vinegar

For the garlicky yogurt

1 cup (250g) Greek yogurt
2 small garlic cloves, grated

For the hot chili butter

7 tablespoons (100g) butter
1 teaspoon hot chili powder
squeeze of lemon juice

Soak the beans in cold water overnight. Drain and rinse them in a colander. Put the beans in a large saucepan, cover with plenty of cold water (no salt), and boil for 50–60 minutes, or until they are cooked but still a little firm in the centers.

Meanwhile, in a large Dutch oven, heat the olive oil over medium-low heat and fry the onions for 10–15 minutes, or until really softened and sweet and going slightly golden. Add the garlic and cook for a further 2–3 minutes, then add 2–3 oregano sprigs and the dried chili flakes and cook for another minute. Add the tomatoes, vinegar, and some black pepper and cook slowly for 20 minutes, or until the sauce has homogenized. Transfer the sauce to a food processor or blender and process until smooth, then return to the same pot. You don't have to purée the sauce but it does turn this into a much more refined dish.

Drain the par-boiled beans, add them to the pot with the remaining oregano sprigs, and cook, partly covered, for 40 minutes, or until the beans are completely cooked.

For the garlicky yogurt, mix together the yogurt and garlic in a small bowl and season well.

Bring a saucepan of salted water to a boil. Poach the eggs for 3 minutes so that the yolks are still soft. Remove each poached egg with a slotted spoon and drain on paper towel.

While the eggs are poaching, make the hot chili butter. Heat a frying pan over high heat, add the butter and chili powder, and cook until the butter starts to go slightly brown and nutty. Carefully add the lemon juice, watching out as it will splutter.

Divide the beans between 4 plates and top each with a poached egg and some of the garlicky yogurt. Drizzle with the hot chili butter to serve.

PREPARATION TIME
15 minutes, plus marinating
(preferably overnight)

COOKING TIME 35-40 minutes

BAKED HALOUMI WITH TAPENADE

Haloumi is the cheese for which even meat-lovers are happy to ditch their meat quota. I guess it's because you can cook haloumi, and it has texture and real bite. It's also salty and takes on flavor very well. We're used to seeing haloumi that's been grilled or pan-fried in slices but my friend Nice gave me a brilliant technique for ramming extra flavor into it: marinate your haloumi and then slowly bake it. Prepared this way the haloumi is permeated with herby, lemony flavor and cooked to the point of almost being goo—but as we know haloumi won't quite go to goo. It's blooming delicious, especially served alongside a tomato and tapenade salad.

....

2 rosemary sprigs
1 tablespoon thyme leaves
a handful of basil leaves
a small handful of flat leaf
    parsley
2 oregano sprigs
zest and juice of 1 lemon
1 tablespoon olive oil
1 x 9oz (250g) block of
    haloumi cheese
freshly ground black pepper
lemon wedges, to serve

For the tapenade

7oz (200g) pitted black olives
1 garlic clove
2 salted anchovy fillets in oil
1 tablespoon chopped flat leaf
    parsley
1 rosemary sprig, chopped
3½ tablespoons (50ml) olive oil

For the tomato salad

3 vine-ripened tomatoes
salt and freshly ground black
    pepper
2 teaspoons sherry vinegar
2 tablespoons olive oil
a small bunch of basil

Place the herbs, lemon zest and juice, and oil in a small blender and process until they form a smooth paste. Alternatively, you can finely chop all the herbs and mix the ingredients together in a bowl. Smear the paste all over the haloumi and season with ground black pepper (definitely don't season with salt, since the haloumi is salty enough). Cover with plastic wrap, put it into the fridge, and leave to marinate for a minimum of 2 hours (though it is actually better to let it marinate overnight).

To make the tapenade, simply put all the ingredients into a small food processor and process until blended.

Preheat the oven to 400°F (200°C). Lay 2 sheets of parchment paper onto a clean countertop. Place the haloumi and its marinade in the center of the paper. Fold the paper up over the haloumi and then fold up the edges to seal them. I use paperclips or staples to seal the parcel together, since you need it to be as airtight as possible. Pop into the oven and bake for 35–40 minutes. This sounds like a long time but you want the whole block of haloumi to be cooked through.

Meanwhile, make the tomato salad by slicing the tomatoes and laying them on a plate. Season with salt and pepper and then drizzle over the vinegar and oil. Finally, drizzle over 2 tablespoons of the tapenade and finish with a scattering of basil leaves.

Serve the haloumi alongside the salad with extra tapenade to dollop and lemon wedges to squeeze over.

PREPARATION TIME
5 minutes, plus cooling

COOKING TIME
15 minutes

ACCIDENTAL TRUFFLE PAPPARDELLE

You know when something great happens completely by mistake? Well, I was developing a recipe for a truffle béarnaise sauce to go with steak and it was good, great in fact, but I had tons of leftover sauce. My mom and I were chatting about how much we love truffles, what they go well with, and how I make my favorite truffle tagliatelli dish (really simply, with a butter emulsion sauce made with the pasta water, butter, and truffle), when suddenly we both slapped our foreheads at the same time, ran into the kitchen, and put some pasta on to cook (all we had was pappardelle). We mixed the hot pasta through the warm truffle béarnaise, topped it with more shaved truffle and some Parmesan, devoured it in seconds, and then did high-kicks around the house because it was so brilliant. So here I give you my accidental truffle pappardelle.

··

Take your hollandaise sauce and stir in the Parmesan, truffle paste, and truffle oil. Allow the sauce to cool a little—it should be warm but not quite room temperature.

Bring a large pan of salted water to a boil and cook the pasta according to the package instructions until al dente. Drain the pasta and then add it to the truffle béarnaise sauce (remember, the sauce should be warm but not hot) and toss through. Serve straightaway with more grated Parmesan and some freshly shaved truffle if you have the bucks.

Hollandaise Sauce (see
  page 215)
½oz (15g) Parmesan cheese,
  grated, plus extra to serve
1 teaspoon white truffle paste
1 teaspoon truffle oil (or more
  if you think it needs it)
11oz (320g) fresh pappardelle
freshly shaved truffle
  (if you fancy it or have the
  cash for it)

VONGOLE WITH BLACK SPAGHETTI & NDUJA

You know when you're asked about your dream ingredient? Mine has to be clams. I can eat them by the bucket-load. Making a classic vongole and melting in nduja or sobrasada (heavily cured, spiced spreadable Spanish sausages a bit like chorizo) makes this dish extra spicy and porky, and its fluorescent orange oil soaks into the black squid-ink spaghetti like a treat.

••

14oz (400g) dried black squid-ink spaghetti
2¼lb (1kg) small clams (check with your fishmonger that they're from sustainable sources), scrubbed clean, discarding any clams that are chipped or open
3½ tablespoons (50ml) extra virgin olive oil
5 garlic cloves, very thinly sliced
1 small dried chili, finely chopped
5oz (150g) nduja or sobrasada sausage, casing removed
1¼ cups (300ml) white wine
a generous squeeze of lemon juice
a small bunch of flat leaf parsley
sea salt flakes and freshly ground black pepper

Cook the spaghetti according to the package instructions in a saucepan of heavily salted boiling water until al dente.

Meanwhile, place a large saucepan with a lid over high heat and let it heat up. Carefully (so not to damage any of the shells) tip the clams into the pan with a splash of water. Put the lid on and let the clams steam in their shells for 1–2 minutes, or until they have all opened (discard any that remain closed). Pour the clams into a sieve over a bowl to collect the cooking liquid.

Quickly wash the saucepan you used to cook the clams. Heat the oil in the clean saucepan over medium heat, then add the garlic and chili and fry for 2–3 minutes, or until the garlic starts to color. Add the nduja or sobrasada and fry until it has completely melted and is starting to get a tiny bit of color. Pour over the white wine and then carefully pour in the clam cooking liquid, making sure to hold back any sand that may have collected at the bottom of the bowl. Cook until this has reduced by half or until it has become "saucey."

While the sauce is reducing, remove the clams from half of the shells (discarding the empty shells). It is a good idea to do this because you need the clam meat but sometimes there are way too many shells for you to be able to mix the whole thing properly. Add the clams (both shelled and unshelled) to the sauce and give it a good stir.

Drain the spaghetti, holding back about 1 tablespoon of the cooking water. Add the pasta to the sauce with the cooking water and clams. Squeeze in the lemon and add the parsley, then thoroughly toss the whole thing together. Season with salt and pepper if it needs it—the clams are very salty—and serve piping hot. Don't forget to serve with finger bowls and a bowl for the empty clamshells.

SERVES 2
···········
PREPARATION TIME
15 minutes

COOKING TIME
45 minutes

ARRABIATA WITH SARDINES & PANGRATTATO

Pantry dinners don't get better than this. And it's true—just because something is not made with entirely fresh ingredients doesn't mean it's bad quality. In fact, I couldn't make this better with fresh stuff. Really great anchovies, olive oil, jarred plum tomatoes, olives, and even the jarred sardines are what make this dish taste so good and the pangrattato (poor man's Parmesan) is a brilliant way to use up leftover bread. This simple tomato sauce needs a slow cook to get the right sweetness from the tomatoes.

···

drizzle of oil
5–6 garlic cloves, finely
  chopped
1 rosemary sprig
½ teaspoon dried chilies,
  crushed
4 salted anchovies in oil
scant 1 cup (200ml) white wine
23oz (650g) great-quality
  canned or jarred plum
  tomatoes (I like to use
  jarred, but by all means use
  canned), whizzed into a purée
handful of basil leaves, plus
  extra to garnish
3½oz (100g) purple olives (such
  as Kalamata), pitted
sea salt flakes and freshly
  ground black pepper
pinch of sugar (optional)
1 x 10oz (300g) jar or can of
  best-quality sardines
6oz (180g) long thin pasta, such
  as linguine, spaghetti, or
  bucatini

For the pangrattato

2 tablespoons olive oil
2 garlic cloves, bashed
1 slice of bread, crusts
  removed and blended into
  crumbs in a food processor
zest of ½ lemon

Make the pangrattato. Heat the oil and garlic in a frying pan over medium heat and fry until the garlic is tinged golden brown. Remove the garlic from the pan and discard. Add the breadcrumbs and lemon zest and slowly toast the crumbs over low heat until they turn a faint golden brown. Remove from the heat, drain on paper towel, and set aside for later.

Heat a drizzle of oil in a large saucepan and gently cook the garlic and rosemary for 2–3 minutes. Remove the rosemary and discard. Add the chilies and anchovies and cook until the anchovies melt into the oil. Pour in the white wine and puréed tomatoes, stir in half the basil, cover, and simmer over medium heat for 20 minutes. Add the olives and cook for a further 10 minutes, or until the sauce has reduced and thickened. Season to taste with salt and pepper and add a pinch of sugar if necessary. Remove from the heat, lay the sardine fillets on top of the pasta sauce, cover with a lid, and leave to warm through for 3 minutes. Don't stir the sardines through the sauce, since it's nice to have the whole fish on top of the dish. I try to keep one side silver, since it's pretty.

Cook the pasta in a large saucepan of salted boiling water for 1 minute less than the package's suggested cooking time, or until al dente. Drain the pasta.

Carefully remove the sardines from the sauce. Stir the pasta and the remaining basil through the sauce. Divide between 2 plates and serve topped with a few sardine fillets, a tablespoon of the pangrattato, and extra basil leaves.

SMOKED MACKEREL & CAULIFLOWER RICE KEDGEREE

SERVES 2

PREPARATION TIME
20 minutes

COOKING TIME
20 minutes

3 tablespoons oil (I use
  coconut oil and it works
  really well)
2 onions, 1½ thinly sliced and
  ½ chopped
3–4 garlic cloves, chopped
1in (3cm) piece of fresh ginger
  root, peeled and chopped
1 red chili (deseeded if you
  don't want it to be too
  spicy), finely chopped
½ teaspoon ground turmeric
½ teaspoon ground cumin
½ teaspoon ground coriander
pinch of ground cloves or
  1 clove
2 free-range eggs (I use
  pasture-raised eggs because
  they have bright orange yolks)
1 small cauliflower, about ¾lb
  (340g), cut into chunks
1 cup (250ml) fresh White
  Chicken Stock (see page 212)
2 smoked mackerel fillets
a small bunch of fresh
  cilantro, roughly chopped
½ small bunch of mint, leaves
  picked and roughly chopped
½ tablespoon fresh lemon juice
sea salt flakes and freshly
  ground black pepper
2 tablespoons flaked almonds,
  toasted

To serve

Greek yogurt
lemon wedges

Now that I've gone batty over cauliflower rice (see page 214) I am looking for ways to incorporate it into recipes. My first step was to look at which things go with cauliflower, then other rice dishes. So, here we go: cauliflower is brilliant with curry, with smoked fish, and with eggs (among other things), so one rice dish that was glaringly obvious to try was kedgeree. And my god, cauliflower rice makes a brilliant one. I'm still genuinely flabbergasted by cauliflower rice: how filling, quick to cook, and genuinely deelish it is. I could shout about it all day long. My kedgeree simplifies everything and is made with ingredients you can get everywhere.

You will need 2 pans: a frying pan and either a sauté pan or a wok with a lid. Heat 1 tablespoon of oil in the frying pan. Add the thinly sliced onions and cook over very low heat for 15 minutes, until the onions become caramelized and faintly crisp. Drain on paper towel and set aside.

While the onions are cooking, you need to make your curry paste. Put the chopped onion, garlic, ginger, chili, and spices in a food processor and process until they form a paste. Heat the remaining oil in the sauté pan or wok. When it is hot, add the paste and cook for 5 minutes over lowish heat until is has completely softened, started to turn golden, and lost its liquid content.

Bring a small saucepan of water to a boil. Add the eggs and boil them for 6 minutes. Drain and then place under cold running water to stop the eggs cooking. Peel the eggs and set aside.

Meanwhile, put the cauliflower into the food processor (I don't bother cleaning it after making the curry paste) and pulse until it resembles something the size of large couscous.

Once the curry paste has cooked, add the cauliflower to the paste in the sauté pan or wok. Stir-fry over high heat for 2 minutes, or until each cauliflower grain is coated. Pour in the chicken stock and add a pinch of salt. Stir and then put a lid on top and cook for 4 minutes. Lay the mackerel, skin-side up, on top, press it down gently so the fish is immersed into the "rice," then put the lid back on and cook for another 3 minutes over lowish heat.

Remove the lid and continue to cook to let some of that liquid reduce. You can peel the skin off the mackerel while this is happening. When there is only about 2 tablespoons of liquid left in the pan and the "rice' is tender, remove from the heat. Add one-third of the caramelized onions, the cilantro and mint (saving a tiny bit for a garnish), and the lemon juice and mix well. Season well. You can break the mackerel up into the kedgeree, if you like, or serve it on top.

Divide between 2 plates. Scatter with the almonds and then the remaining caramelized onions. Cut the eggs in half (they should have slightly gooey middles) and then place 2 egg halves on top of each serving. Garnish with the remaining herbs and serve with Greek yogurt and lemon wedges.

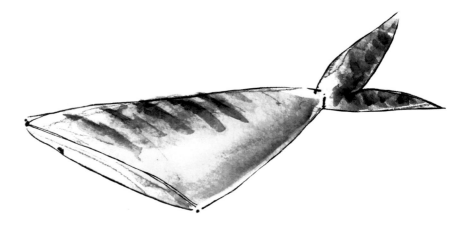

SERVES 2
....

PREPARATION TIME
25 minutes, plus proving
overnight

COOKING TIME 30 minutes

ROASTED FENNEL &
SAUSAGE CALZONE

2 large fennel bulbs, thinly
  sliced, fronds reserved
1 tablespoon sherry vinegar
  (red or white wine vinegar
  would also be great)
3 tablespoons olive oil
sea salt flakes and freshly
  ground black pepper
3 sausages (I use Italian
  fennel ones but you could use
  any herby pork sausages)
5oz (150g) mozzarella cheese
3oz (80g) pepperoni or cured
  fennel salami, sliced
a good pinch of fennel seeds,
  toasted
a good pinch of dried chili
  flakes

For the dough

2 cups (300g) white bread flour
  or Italian "00" flour
¼oz (7g) envelope of instant or
  fast-acting dry yeast
1 tablespoon sugar
scant ½ cup (100ml) lukewarm
  water
1 tablespoon salt
2 tablespoons olive oil

For the tomato sauce

3 tablespoons olive oil
3 garlic cloves, very finely
  chopped
1 basil sprig
1¾ cups (400ml) tomato passata
  or purée (I make my own by
  blending a 14oz/400g can of
  cherry tomatoes)
a splash of sherry or red wine
  vinegar
pinch of sugar

What's not to love about calzone? It's essentially a pizza that's been folded and made into a turnover but it's stuffed double-full with filling. Making your own pizza dough is a pain in the bum and I'm not one of those chefs who's going to say otherwise. Making dough is therapeutic, for sure, but it takes ages to rise, it's hard to know when it's the right consistency, and it can be temperamental. I suggest you make the dough the day before and let it rise slowly in the fridge, which means you'll only need to make the fillings and bake the calzone on the day.
So let's get chatting about this particular calzone.
All the greats are in it: the fennel bulbs, seeds, and fronds are utter sex when paired with the pork and spice from the fresh sausages and cured pepperoni. This alone makes the whole process worthwhile.

....

The day before you want to cook the calzone, make the dough. Add the flour, yeast, and sugar to a large bowl, stir well, and slowly mix in the water, salt, and oil. Knead the dough well for 10 minutes. You can do this in a stand mixer with a dough hook for ease. Place the dough in an oiled bowl, cover tightly with plastic wrap, followed by a warm, damp cloth, and leave to rise for 2 hours. Knock the dough back, then cover the bowl with oiled plastic wrap and leave in the fridge overnight. This is actually a better way to rise dough, giving it first a fast rise and then a slow one; it allows the yeast to mellow a bit so that the dough doesn't taste so yeasty.

To make the tomato sauce, heat the oil in a small saucepan, add the garlic and basil, and fry gently for 1–2 minutes, or until aromatic and softened but not going too golden. Pour in the passata, vinegar, and sugar and cook slowly for about 15 minutes, or until thickened. A good indication that the sauce is ready is when the oil starts to split a little. Season with salt and pepper and process in a blender or with an immersion blender to make a smooth sauce.

Meanwhile, heat your oven to as hot as it will go. My oven goes up to 475°F (250°C) but some only go to 425°F (220°C). Place the fennel in roasting tray and add the vinegar, 2 tablespoons of oil, and some salt and pepper. »

« Roast for about 20 minutes, turning halfway through, until the fennel is cooked all the way through and tinged golden at the edges. Remove from the oven and set aside until it is cool enough to touch.

Heat the remaining oil in a frying pan. Squeeze the sausages out of their skins, breaking some bits into small meatball-sized pieces and some into larger pieces. Fry the sausage meat for 2–3 minutes, or until cooked through and browned.

Divide the dough into 2 balls. Place each ball on a large sheet of parchment paper and roll it out thinly until it forms a circle about 12in (30cm) in diameter. Top each dough circle with one-quarter of the tomato sauce. Then add half the mozzarella, roasted fennel, sausage meat, pepperoni, fennel seeds, and dried chili to each one and season well.

Fold over the dough to make half-moon-shaped parcels, using the parchment paper to help you lift the dough, and crimp the edges together. With your oven still turned up as hot as it will go, cook each calzone for 10 minutes on a pizza stone or a baking sheet, then serve with the remaining sauce poured on top and fennel fronds to garnish.

PREPARATION TIME
25 minutes, plus cooling
and marinating overnight
COOKING TIME 1 hour

MARINATED MACKEREL, BABY BEETS & HORSERADISH CRÈME FRAÎCHE

My mom is half Polish and she loves a rollmop. Because of this, naturally, so do I! I tested this recipe with herrings first and it works really well but there is something about the firm flesh and oiliness of mackerel that takes so well to pickling. So here I have pickled mackerel with horseradish and beets. These flavors are all very classic but I've made a bit more of the marinade by adding in some dried chilies and lemon juice.

....

To make the marinade, place ¼ cup (70ml) water and the vinegar, bay leaf, lemon rind, lemon juice, peppercorns, chilies, allspice berries, sugar, and salt in a small pan and heat slowly until everything melts together. Bring to a boil and then turn off the heat. Add the onion and carrot and then leave to cool.

Lay the mackerel fillets in a dish and pour the marinade over them, making sure they are completely immersed. Cover with plastic wrap and leave in the fridge to marinate overnight.

Preheat the oven to 375°F (190°C). Wrap each beet variety seperately in foil with a splash of water and some salt and roast for 1 hour, or until just tender. Once cooked, allow to cool in the foil and then peel and trim the beets. I like a little bit of the "hair" left on them. Mix together the lemon juice and oil with plenty of seasoning in a small bowl. Place each beet variety in a separate bowl and dress each bowl with one-third of the dressing. Leave to marinate for 1 hour. Just before serving you can mix the beets together.

In a small bowl, mix together the horseradish, crème fraîche, and lemon juice and add plenty of seasoning.

To serve, add a blob of the horseradish crème fraîche on the side of each plate, lay 2 pieces of mackerel alongside, place the beet salad on top of the horseradish crème fraîche, and garnish with some watercress.

1½ cups (350ml) white wine vinegar
1 bay leaf
the rind, cut into strips, and juice of 1 lemon
1 teaspoon black peppercorns
½ teaspoon dried chili flakes or 3–4 small dried chilies
½ teaspoon allspice berries
¼ cup (50g) sugar
1½ tablespoons table salt
1 onion, thinly sliced into rings
1 carrot, thinly sliced
4 mackerel, filleted (I like the tails left on)
a bunch of watercress, to garnish

For the beet salad

5oz (150g) baby candy-stripe beets
5oz (150g) baby golden beets
5oz (150g) baby purple beets
3 tablespoons lemon juice
3 tablespoons olive oil
sea salt flakes and freshly ground black pepper

For the horseradish crème fraîche

2 tablespoons horseradish (freshly grated or sauce)
5 tablespoons crème fraîche
1 tablespoon lemon juice

SPICE

CHILIES & WARMTH

SERVES 2
....

PREPARATION TIME
20 minutes, plus marinating

COOKING TIME
50 minutes

HARISSA SHRIMP WITH CAULIFLOWER COUSCOUS & ROASTED VEGETABLES

8–10 big fat raw jumbo shrimp, peeled, deveined, and slit deeply down the backs with the tails left on
½ teaspoon sea salt flakes
2 tablespoons olive oil
½ teaspoon ground cumin
½ teaspoon ground coriander
1 tablespoon harissa
3 garlic cloves, finely chopped
juice of 1 lemon

For the cauliflower couscous & roasted vegetables

1 small orange-fleshed pumpkin or winter squash (such as Munchkin, Golden Nugget, or onion squash), halved, deseeded, and cut into 8 wedges with the skin on
1 zucchini, halved and then cut into 6 pieces
1 red pepper
3 tablespoons olive oil
sea salt flakes and freshly ground black pepper
½lb (250g) cauliflower, trimmed and then cut into pieces
scant ½ cup (100ml) fresh White Chicken Stock (see page 212)
1 tablespoon lemon juice
a small package (about 1oz/30g) of cilantro, roughly chopped
a small package (about 1oz/30g) of flat leaf parsley, roughly chopped
½ small package (about ½oz/15g) of mint, leaves picked and roughly chopped
2 tablespoons mixed seeds, toasted
1 tablespoon pine nuts, toasted

To serve

generous ½ cup (150g) plain yogurt
1 tablespoon rose harissa

Cauliflower rice resembles couscous more than it does rice, so I had to try it out in that guise. The thing that wrecks my head about this whole thing is that cauliflower is a great vehicle for flavor in much the same way as many starchier carbohydrates. Cauliflower couscous slurps up flavors and is almost more filling than the real deal. Here I've served it with marinated harissa shrimp that are quickly cooked. Damn straight, this is delicious.

....

Place the shrimp in a non-reactive bowl with the salt, oil, cumin, coriander, harissa, and garlic. Cover with plastic wrap and leave to marinate in the fridge for between 30–60 minutes while you get on with the rest of the recipe.

Heat the oven to 400°F (200°C). Place the pumpkin, zucchini, and whole red pepper in a roasting tray, rub with 1 tablespoon of the oil, and then season with tons of salt and pepper. (There's no need to add any spices to the vegetables, since the harissa in the marinade is genuinely sufficient when the whole dish is put together later on.) Put this in the oven and roast for 45 minutes, turning the vegetables halfway through, until the vegetables are a little charred and cooked through. Remove from the oven and set aside.

Put the red pepper in a plastic bag, seal the bag, and leave to steam for 5 minutes. This will make the skin easier to peel away from the pepper's flesh. When the 5 minutes are up, take the pepper out of the bag, pull out the stalk, cut the pepper in half, and remove the seeds. Peel away the skin and then slice each half pepper into 4 pieces.

While the vegetables are roasting, make the cauliflower couscous. Place the cauliflower in a food processor and pulse until it resembles something the size of couscous. Heat 1 tablespoon of oil in a frying pan with a lid and then throw in the cauliflower. Cook over high heat for 1 minute to sear the outside of the cauliflower, stirring continuously to keep it moving—you do not want it to color. Pour in the stock, add some salt, and then put the lid on. Cook for 5 minutes, then remove the lid and cook it down until the stock has reduced into the rice.

Transfer the cauliflower couscous to a serving dish. Whisk together the lemon juice and 1 tablespoon of oil with some salt and pepper. Pour this dressing over the cauliflower. Add the herbs and mix well, then add the roasted vegetables, mixed seeds, and pine nuts and give it a really good mix. Leave to stand for 5 minutes and let the flavors homogenize while you make the yogurt sauce and cook the shrimp.

To make the yogurt sauce, spoon the yogurt into a serving bowl, add the harissa, and season with salt and pepper. Swirl together and set aside.

Heat a frying pan until almost smoking. Lay the shrimp on their sides around the pan and fry for 1 minute or until the cooked sides are a little charred. Flip the shrimp over and cook for another minute or until the other sides are lightly charred and the shrimp are pink. Give the shrimp a good stir-fry around the pan, then add the lemon juice to the pan and stir the shrimp quickly so they caramelize in the juice. Top the cauliflower couscous and roasted vegetables with the shrimp, and serve with the yogurt sauce on the side.

WAT TAN HOR

The first time that I ate this dish was at a street food stall in Borneo. I was being really nosey and I saw that all the tourists were eating nasi goreng and all the Chinese Malaysians were eating wat tan hor. It looks like a mess but it's so damn good. It's fresh ho fun noodles fried in soy and oyster sauce with seafood poached in a simple fresh chicken stock thickened with cornstarch and egg. I eat this at least once a month at C&R Café in Chinatown in London. You really need to use fresh noodles, which you can buy from Chinatown or a Chinese supermarket. I've tried making this dish with rehydrated noodles and although it works (so use them if you really can't source fresh ones), it's not quite the same. I turned to my food writer friend Lizzie Mabbott (who blogs under the name of Hollow Legs) for help with this recipe because there are so many ways you can do it. She helped me to understand that you poach the seafood and that the sauce is very plain, which I couldn't quite believe, and gave me the tip to use unsmoked bacon, since it's not easy to find thinly sliced pork belly. I spent so much time in Thailand when I was growing up that I always like to finish my wat tan hor with a spicy soy sauce that's made in the same way that the Thais would make nam pla (spicy fish sauce).

....

a package of fresh ho fun noodles (from the refrigerated aisle at a Chinese supermarket)
table salt
3 tablespoons cooking oil
1 tablespoon dark soy sauce
1½ tablespoons light soy sauce
1 tablespoon oyster sauce
2 very thin slices of pork belly (or you could use unsmoked streaky bacon), chopped into 1in (3cm) slices
4 garlic cloves, minced
1 teaspoon peeled and grated fresh ginger root
1 small squid, cleaned and sliced into rings
10 raw jumbo shrimp
½ fish cake, sliced thinly, or 6 fish balls, halved
2 cups (500ml) fresh White Chicken Stock (see page 212)
a generous pinch of sugar
a pinch of white pepper
a small package (about 9oz/ 250g) of choi sum or bok choi
3 tablespoons cornstarch mixed with 3 tablespoons water
2 free-range eggs, beaten

For the chili & soy sauce

4 Thai red chilies, thinly sliced
¼–½ cup soy sauce

To make the chili and soy sauce, mix together the chilies and the soy sauce in a bowl and set aside.

Soak the ho fun noodles in a bowl of hot water with a good pinch of salt and separate the noodle strands carefully with chopsticks or your fingers. Drain the noodles and rinse under cold running water, then plunge the noodles into a bowl of ice-cold water so they don't stick together. Just before using, drain the noodles and pat them dry.

Heat a wok with 1 tablespoon of oil and fry the noodles with both the soy and oyster sauces until the noodles are covered with the sauces and start to get some caramelization. Divide the noodles between 4 serving plates or, more preferably, pasta plates with high sides.

Wipe out the wok with paper towel, then add 1 tablespoon of cooking oil and fry the pork for 1–2 minutes over high heat until the fat starts to render away and the meat takes on a golden color. Add the garlic and ginger and fry for another minute. Transfer to a bowl and set side.

Now heat up the remaining oil in the wok until fiery hot and fry the squid, shrimp, and fish cake or balls for few minutes. Add the fried pork and toss it around, then add the stock, sugar, white pepper, and whichever greens you are using and simmer for 2–3 minutes, or until the fish is poached. Whisk in the cornstarch mixture until the sauce has thickened to a gravy-like consistency. Turn off the heat and drizzle in the eggs, stirring as you go so that you get strands of egg suspended in the sauce. Pour this over the noodles and serve immediately with some of the chili and soy sauce poured over, if you like.

SERVES 2
....

PREPARATION TIME
10 minutes

COOKING TIME
10 minutes

HOME-STYLE CABBAGE

This was inspired by a dish from a brilliant Sichuan restaurant in Camberwell, London. It's just stir-fried cabbage but it's so blinking delicious that I could eat it for breakfast, lunch, and dinner. The restaurant won't spill the details about how to make it, so I put my head together with brilliant food writers Helen Graves and Lizzie Mabbott and came up with this recipe. I like to use a normal green cabbage but actually it should be made with Chinese cabbage. I'll leave it to you to decide which type of cabbage to use.

....

Mix the sauce ingredients together in a small bowl and set aside.

Blanch the cabbage in a saucepan of boiling water for 30 seconds if using green cabbage or 10 seconds if using Chinese cabbage. Drain and quickly plunge into a bowl of iced water.

Heat 2 tablespoons of oil in a wok over medium heat. Add the garlic, scallions, Sichuan pepper, and chilies and fry for 1 minute. Remove and set aside.

Drain the blanched cabbage. Put the wok back on the burner, turn the heat up to the maximum, and add the remaining oil. Once the wok is literally smoking hot, quickly add the blanched cabbage and stir-fry until heated through. Add the sauce and return the fried garlic, scallions, Sichuan pepper, and chilies to the wok. Mix well and cook for about 30 seconds, or until the sauce has thickened. Serve immediately. I would eat this simply with either white or brown rice for extra fiber.

11b (500g) green cabbage or
  Napa (Chinese) cabbage,
  chopped into large pieces
3 tablespoons vegetable oil
3 garlic cloves, finely chopped
2 scallions (white and green
  parts), thinly sliced
½ teaspoon Sichuan
  peppercorns, crushed
3 dried chilies, deseeded and
  cut into small pieces

For the sauce

3 tablespoons Chinkiang
  vinegar (black rice vinegar)
2 tablespoons light soy sauce
1 tablespoon sugar
1 teaspoon salt
1 rounded teaspoon cornstarch
2 tablespoons water

················

PREPARATION TIME
15 minutes, plus soaking overnight

COOKING TIME 2¼ hours

PULLED CHIPOTLE CHICKEN WITH PINK PICKLED ONIONS

1 cup (200g) dried adzuki beans
2 tablespoons olive oil
1 medium, whole, free-range chicken, jointed
sea salt flakes and freshly ground black pepper
2 onions, thinly sliced
1 bulb of garlic, cut in half horizontally
2-3 dried chipotle chilies, rehydrated for 10 minutes in 3½ tablespoons (50ml) boiling water
1 cinnamon stick
4 cloves
1 tablespoon ground cumin
1 tablespoon ground coriander
2 teaspoons smoked paprika
1lb (500g) chopped fresh tomatoes
2 cups (500ml) fresh White Chicken Stock (see page 212)
2 bay leaves

To serve

Cauliflower Rice (see page 214)
Pink Pickled Onions (see page 131)
½ avocado, peeled, pitted, and chopped and dressed with a squeeze of lime juice and a sprinkling of salt
3½oz (130g) mixed bean sprouts and sprouted lentils, dressed with a little of the Pink Pickled Onion juice

I wanted to make a chicken variation of chili. It's not that I believe that red meat is bad for you but for midweek, when you're pushed for time and on an "eating lighter" vibe, chicken cooks more quickly and is lower in calories. I've chopped up a whole chicken for this recipe—I honestly feel that it's better value, better for the environment, and weirdly therapeutic. It's possibly the most fun kitchen skill, but if you don't want to do this then just buy chicken pieces on the bone. I've also used dried and cooked adzuki beans, which remind me of mini red kidney beans, but a good cheat would be to use a 14oz (400g) can of adzuki beans or actual red kidney beans. Adzuki beans are full of dietary fiber and disease-fighting flavonoids. So on with the recipe. Chipotle chilies (dried and smoked jalapeños that have a deep spicy and smoky flavor) are essential and now available in most supermarkets and online. This recipe shows that healthy eating can be as good as, if not better than, being indulgent—and this dish is so good that it could even be cooked for entertaining.

Place the adzuki beans in a bowl, cover with a good few inches of cold water, and leave to soak for 4–12 hours or overnight if you can, then boil in fresh water for 1 hour.

Heat the oil over high heat in a large saucepan. Season the chicken pieces and then brown them in batches. It's important that you get really good color on the chicken pieces and render down the fat, since this is where the base flavor of the stew will come from. Once the chicken is browned, set it aside on a plate.

Lower the heat, add the onions to the same pan, and fry them very slowly for 10–15 minutes, making sure to scrape up all the chicken residue at the bottom of the pan with a wooden spoon, until the onions have really softened, sweetened, and turned a bit golden. While frying the onions, push them to one side of the pan and make space for the garlic bulb halves. Fry the garlic until the cut sides get a bit of color, then remove the garlic and set aside with the chicken.

»

«   Once the onions are ready, increase the heat, add all the spices, and fry them for a further 2 minutes. Next, add in the chopped tomatoes and give it a good stir. Put a lid on the pan and cook for 2 minutes, or until the steam has started to break the tomatoes up. Now you can remove the lid and turn the heat back down. Cook for a further 10 minutes. The idea is to reduce the tomatoes until they are a really rich and thick tomato sauce.

Pour in the stock, stir, and then return the chicken pieces and garlic bulb halves to the pan and add the bay leaves. Cover with a lid and cook for 30 minutes. Drain the adzuki beans, add them to the pan, and cook for another 20 minutes. Remove the chicken from the pan and set aside while you reduce the sauce. Cook the sauce until the flavor is rich and strong and the sauce has thickened.

Meanwhile, use two forks to shred the chicken, removing all the bones as you go. When the sauce is ready, return the chicken to the pan, season, and stir well.

Serve the pulled chipotle chicken with the Cauliflower Rice, Pink Pickled Onions, avocado, and the sprouted bean salad.

SERVES 4
·············

PREPARATION TIME
20 minutes

COOKING TIME
25 minutes

MACKEREL FILLETS WITH CURRIED POTATO SALAD, SOFT-BOILED EGGS & HERBS

Okay, so this is not potato salad as we know it. It makes a terrific supper as it is but is equally great for a picnic or take-into-work lunch dish if you let everything cool, swap grilled mackerel for smoked mackerel, and boil your eggs for an extra minute. Either way, it's a heck of a way to eat potatoes and fish!

···

olive oil
1 tablespoon cumin seeds
1 tablespoon curry powder
1¾lb (800g) fingerling or other
    salad potatoes, cut into
    ½in (1cm) slices
sea salt flakes and freshly
    ground black pepper
1½ cups (350ml) fresh White
    Chicken or Fish Stock (see
    pages 212-13, water is also
    fine but you'll have less
    flavor)
2 free-range eggs (I always go
    for pasture-raised eggs,
    since they have bright-
    colored yolks)
a small package (about 1oz/30g)
    of cilantro, leaves picked
a small package (about 1oz/30g)
    of mint, leaves picked
½ package (about ½oz/15g) of
    dill, leaves picked
2 tablespoons chives, cut into
    1in (2cm) lengths
1 tablespoon lemon juice
4 largish mackerel fillets

Heat 1 tablespoon of oil in a medium saucepan with a lid. Add the cumin seeds and gently toast for 1 minute or until aromatic. Add the curry powder and toast for a further 30 seconds. Tip in the potatoes, add a good pinch of salt, and stir to coat thoroughly with the spices. Pour in the stock, then cover and cook the potatoes slowly over low heat for 15 minutes, giving them a stir every now and then. The potatoes shouldn't break up because you're using a waxy salad variety but if they do, fear not, it just means that they will absorb the dressing even better. When the potatoes are cooked, remove from the heat, drain, and leave them to steam in the pan with the lid on for a further 5 minutes (this makes sure they're all evenly cooked throughout). Transfer the potatoes to a mixing bowl and leave to cool a little.

Meanwhile, add the eggs to a saucepan of salted boiling water and cook for 6 minutes. Drain and then place under cold running water until the eggs are cool enough to handle. Peel the eggs: they should be soft but holding their shape well. Dry with paper towel and set aside.

To make the herby salad, place all the picked leaves and the chives in a bowl, then add 2 tablespoons of oil, the lemon juice, and plenty of salt and pepper. Next, pour this over the warm (not hot) curried potatoes and stir well.

Finally, heat a little oil in a frying pan. Season the mackerel fillets with salt and pepper, then place them in the frying pan, skin-side down, and pan-fry over a fierce heat for 2–3 minutes, or until the skin is crisp and golden. Flip over the fish fillets and cook for a further minute.

Cut the boiled eggs in half. Divide the curried potato salad between 4 plates and top the salad with a mackerel fillet and half a boiled egg. Crème fraîche or sour cream would also be a nice addition.

···

PREPARATION TIME
15 minutes

COOKING TIME
10 minutes

THAI CHICKEN FRIED RICE

This is a dish from my youth. When my sisters and I first started going to Thailand we would eat this on the beach pretty much every day. I returned to Thailand recently after a good 15 years and this dish is still served pretty much everywhere. I remember it always having the egg scrambled into it, but more recently it seems to be served like nasi goreng, the Malaysian version of this dish, with a fried egg on top. Thai Chicken Fried Rice is one of my top ten things to eat and cook and it's really quick and easy to make.

••

Bash the garlic and chilies in a mortar and pestle until all the oils burst out of them. This really is better than pulsing them together in a food processor or simply chopping them up but if you're pressed for time or don't have the equipment then you can, by all means, do either of these instead.

Heat the oil in a large wok. Add the eggs and scramble them really quickly, then scoop them out of the pan and set aside on a plate. Next, add the ginger, chilies, and garlic and fry for about 20 seconds, or until they become aromatic. Add the chicken and leave it for 1 minute (instead of stir-frying) to get some color. Flip the chicken over and cook for another minute on the other side. Add the beans and stir-fry for 2 minutes, or until the chicken is cooked through and the beans are tender. Add the rice and stir-fry for 3–4 minutes over really high heat—you want the rice to start to catch a bit on the base of the pan. A minute before the end of cooking time, when you're sure the rice is heated through, stir in the tomatoes, basil, oyster and fish sauces, sugar, and the reserved eggs and cook until combined.

Meanwhile, make the nam pla. Mix together the fish sauce and the chilies and leave to macerate for 1 minute.

Serve the rice with the chopped cucumber, lime wedges and some nam pla.

4 garlic cloves, peeled
2 red Thai bird's eye chilies, chopped
2 tablespoons vegetable oil
2 free-range eggs, beaten
1in (3cm) piece of fresh ginger root, grated
2 skinless, boneless, free-range chicken breasts, chopped into large bite-sized chunks
5oz (150g) long beans or string beans, cut into 1in (3cm) pieces
2 cups (400g) Thai Jasmine rice (or basmati rice), cooked and chilled
15 cherry tomatoes, halved
a good handful of Thai basil, plus extra to garnish
2 tablespoons oyster sauce
1 tablespoon Thai fish sauce
2 teaspoons sugar
½ cucumber, peeled, deseeded, and chopped diagonally
lime wedges, to serve

For the nam pla

3 tablespoons fish sauce
4 Thai red chilies, thinly sliced

SERVES 4
....

PREPARATION TIME
30 minutes

COOKING TIME
50 minutes

GREEN MOLE IN TORTILLA BASKETS WITH RICE, BEANS & MEXICAN SALAD

2 onions, 1 quartered and
   1 finely chopped
6 garlic cloves, 2 left whole
   and 4 finely chopped
5 black peppercorns
10 cloves
1 cinnamon stick
1 whole, medium, free-range
   chicken, cut into pieces,
   skin removed
1 tablespoon olive oil
3½oz (100g) pumpkin seeds,
   ground to dust in a food
   processor
1 green pepper (a poblano if
   you can find one), cored,
   deseeded, and chopped
2 green chilies, chopped
a handful of cilantro leaves
2 tarragon sprigs
2 flat leaf parsley sprigs
3oz (80g) baby spinach (about
   2½ cups)
just under 1lb fresh green
   tomatoes or 1 x 14oz (400g)
   can tomatillos (from the
   Mexican food aisle of a
   supermarket)
sea salt flakes and freshly
   ground black pepper

For the tortilla baskets

4 good-quality, large corn
   tortillas
olive oil in a spray

To serve

1 cup (200g) basmati rice,
   cooked
1 x 14oz (400g) can black beans,
   drained
1 avocado, peeled, pitted,
   chopped, and dressed with
   some lemon or lime juice
1 Little Gem lettuce, shredded
cilantro leaves

I was introduced to green mole while I was in LA learning about Mexican food and its ingredients. Green mole is thickened with seeds and flavored with herbs, chilies, and green peppers. It's lighter and way more delicious than its more famous brother that's famously finished with chocolate. The tortilla baskets are a bit of fun. Make them if you can be bothered, but the dish is just as delicious served over plain, boiled rice.

Put the quartered onion, whole garlic cloves, whole spices, and chicken pieces into a saucepan and cover with cold water. Bring to a boil, then reduce to a simmer and cook for 25 minutes, or until the chicken pieces are cooked through and tender. Strain the chicken, reserving the stock and discarding the vegetables and spices. Use 2 forks to shred the chicken pieces and set aside.

Heat the oil in a large frying pan over high heat. Add the chopped onion, then lower the heat and fry for 10 minutes until softened and lightly golden, adding the chopped garlic for the final minute. Add the pumpkin seeds, green pepper, and green chilies and fry for another minute, then add the cilantro, tarragon, parsley, spinach, tomatoes or tomatillos, and 1¼ cups (300ml) of the reserved chicken stock and cook the sauce for about 30 minutes, until the tomatoes have completely broken up and the sauce has reduced.

Transfer the sauce to a blender and blend until smooth. Pass the sauce through a sieve into a clean pan and add the shredded chicken. Bring to a boil and season to taste with salt and pepper. The green mole stew should be a little thicker than a Thai curry.

Meanwhile, make the tortilla baskets. Preheat the oven to 400°F (200°C). Spritz the corn tortillas on both sides with the olive oil spray, then tuck them into 4 small to medium tapas dishes or ramekins. Bake the tortillas for 8 minutes, or until crisped up. If you don't have 4 dishes you can do this in batches—the baskets don't have to be served hot. To serve, split the rice between each tortilla basket, then top with some green mole stew, some black beans, avocado, shredded lettuce, and cilantro leaves.

PREPARATION TIME
25 minutes

COOKING TIME
1½ hours

GREEN CHILI WITH GREEN APPLE SALSA

You really need to use tomatillos (Mexican husk tomatoes) for this chile verde but in their absence tomatoes are fine.

Blacken and blister the pepper skin over a direct flame on the stovetop or under the broiler. Put them in a plastic food bag for 10 minutes while still hot—this will make the skins easier to peel. Peel the skins off the peppers, then halve them and remove the seeds. Roughly chop the flesh and set aside.

Heat 2 tablespoons of olive oil in a large saucepan over medium heat. Add the ground pork in batches and a good pinch of salt and pepper. Cook for a good few minutes until browned, stirring occasionally. It's really important to get a good amount of color on the meat for a strong meaty flavor. Remove the meat with a slotted spoon and transfer to a bowl.

In the same pan add the remaining oil, then add the onions and fry for 10–15 minutes over medium heat until soft— for the last 2 minutes add in the garlic and chilies. Add the cumin seeds and fry for 1–2 minutes, then add the ground coriander. Return the meat to the pan and continue cooking for another 5 minutes. Stir in the tomatillos or green tomatoes and the peppers and then pour in the stock. Reduce the heat to low and leave to bubble for about 1 hour.

Before serving, blend all the herbs together in a blender with a pinch of salt and a splash of water until you have a green paste. Squeeze in the lime, then stir this into the meat. Scatter on the remaining herbs and serve with warm tortillas, sour cream, shredded lettuce, and Green Apple Salsa.

2 green peppers
3 tablespoons olive oil
1¾lb (800g) ground pork (if you buy from a butcher ask for a single coarse grind)
sea salt flakes and freshly ground black pepper
2 onions, roughly chopped
3 garlic cloves, finely sliced
4 hot green chilies, roughly chopped
2 tablespoons cumin seeds
2 teaspoons ground coriander
6-8 large tomatillos or green tomatoes, roughly chopped or 2 x 12oz (350g) cans tomatillos
1⅔ cups (400ml) fresh White Chicken Stock (see page 212)
½ large bunch each of parsley, cilantro, and oregano, leaves picked (save a few leaves for the garnish)
juice of 1 lime

To serve

4 flour tortillas, warmed
⅔ cup (150ml) sour cream
1 Little Gem lettuce, shredded
Green Apple Salsa (see right)

GREEN APPLE SALSA

1 Granny Smith apple, finely chopped
a handful of cilantro, roughly chopped
2 scallions, very finely chopped
¼ teaspoon finely chopped green chili
juice of 1 lime

Simply combine all the ingredients in a small bowl and season to taste. Leave to macerate for about 30 minutes before serving to get all the flavors in harmony.

SERVES 4
....

PREPARATION TIME
20 minutes

COOKING TIME
1½ hours

DHAL WITH SPICED HEIRLOOM CARROTS, TOFU & CASHEWS

When I'm in a slump, a warming bowl of dhal is the thing that will cheer me up. I make dhal a lot, mostly because it's a pantry-staple dish and I've always got the base ingredients on hand. The base of this dhal is pretty classic, though it may seem weird having to blend sesame seeds with spices—they act as flavor, but also as an enricher for a really creamy finish. Then we roast a whole bunch of multicolored heritage carrots, some tofu, and cashew nuts and serve them on top for a more complete dinner. I serve this with cauliflower rice for an even bigger nutritional punch.

....

To make the dhal, bash the mustard seeds, cumin seeds, coriander seeds, sesame seeds, and chili flakes together in a mortar and pestle, or use a spice grinder. Heat 1 teaspoon of oil over low heat in a large saucepan. Add the onions and fry very slowly for about 20 minutes, or until they have really softened and start to turn golden brown. Add the garlic, turmeric, ginger, and chili and fry for 2 minutes, then add the spices and fry for 1 minute. Add the lentils to the pan and stir to coat them in the spices. Cover with the stock and coconut milk and bring to a boil, then lower the heat and simmer for 30 minutes. Season with plenty of salt and black pepper.

Preheat the oven to 400°F (200°C). Put the carrots in a baking dish. Mix the coconut oil together with the cumin seeds, chili flakes, and plenty of salt and pepper, then rub over the carrots. Roast for 30–35 minutes, stirring halfway through. For the last 15 minutes of roasting, put the tofu and the cashew nuts into the dish with the carrots and swiftly coat in the spices. Place back in the oven, turning the tofu after 10 minutes.

Serve the dhal in bowls, each topped with tofu, roasted carrots, some cashews, and fresh cilantro, alongside Cauliflower Rice.

1¾lb (800g) heritage (multicolored) chantenay or other small, thick carrots, peeled
1 tablespoon coconut oil
1 teaspoon cumin seeds
½ teaspoon chili flakes
4 x ½in (1cm) slices of firm tofu

Dhal base

1 tablespoon black mustard seeds
1 tablespoon cumin seeds
1 tablespoon coriander seeds
1 tablespoon white sesame seeds
¼ teaspoon dried chili flakes
2 teaspoons vegetable oil
2 onions, chopped
6 garlic cloves, grated
a thumb-sized piece of fresh turmeric, grated, or 1 tablespoon ground turmeric
a thumb-sized piece of fresh ginger root, grated
1 red chili, finely chopped
½ cup (100g) red lentils
2 cups (500ml) fresh White Chicken or Veggie Stock (see pages 212–13)
1 x 14oz (400ml) can coconut milk
sea salt flakes and freshly ground black pepper

To serve

3½oz (100g) cashew nuts
a handful of fresh cilantro leaves
Cauliflower Rice (see page 214)

SWEET

DELICIOUS TREATS

BLACK VELVET CAKE

I remember first trying Nigella Lawson's chocolate Guinness cake like it was yesterday. I was testing it for a magazine feature over 10 years ago, and it blew my mind—by far the best chocolate cake I had ever made or eaten, and it wasn't slathered in chocolate icing. The contrast of dense, sticky, chocolaty, and mildly boozy sponge cake with sharp and creamy cream cheese frosting was an instant win. So much so that when I started my website I did a homage to Nigella's cake, but added real chocolate (Nigella only uses cocoa powder) and switched the Guinness to chocolate stout. Now, here's when it gets a bit weird. My best friend Zoe and I tend to drink in hotel rooms and sing Karaoke off YouTube; by tradition, we start with "Black Velvet" by Alannah Myles. This got me thinking: I wear black velvet A LOT, I love the song A LOT, I love the drink A LOT, I like red velvet cake A LOT; is it possible to merge all these things into one? Well, I damn well gave it a good try, and I give you my black velvet cake—the best cake you will EVER MAKE— dedicated to my "wifey." It's indulgent reducing a bottle of champagne down to syrup, so feel free to use Cava or prosecco.

2¼ sticks (250g) unsalted butter, chopped into cubes, plus extra for greasing
1 cup (250ml) chocolate stout or Guinness
3½oz (100g) bittersweet chocolate (70% cocoa solids), broken into pieces
heaped ¼ cup (35g) cocoa powder
2 cups (400g) superfine sugar
2 eggs
⅔ cup (142g) plain yogurt
1 tablespoon vanilla extract
2 cups (275g) all-purpose flour
2½ tablespoons baking soda

For the frosting

1 x 750ml bottle of champagne
2 x 8oz packages (225g) cream cheese
1¾ cups (200g) confectioner's sugar
1 cup (250ml) heavy cream

Preheat the oven to 350°F (180°C). Butter and line the base and sides of a 9in (23cm) diameter, deep, round, springform pan.

Melt the butter together with the Guinness in a large saucepan, then add the chocolate. Once the chocolate has melted, add the cocoa powder and sugar and mix well.

In a separate bowl, whisk together the eggs, yogurt, and vanilla extract, then add this to the chocolate mixture. Whisk in the flour and baking soda and whisk well until you have a smooth batter. Pour this mixture into the pan and bake for 45 minutes. If a knife comes out clean, it's done. Leave to cool in the pan.

Meanwhile, to make the icing, pour the champagne into a saucepan, bring to a boil, and reduce it down until you only have 2 tablespoons left. Leave to cool completely before adding it into the cream cheese.

In a large bowl, lightly whip the cream cheese with the confectioner's sugar and champagne reduction until smooth.

In a separate bowl, whip the cream until it thickens but still retains its shape. Fold the cream into the cream cheese mixture until it is smooth and a spreadable consistency. I like to chill it for an hour or two while the cake is cooking and cooling.

Remove the cake from the pan. If the top is still a little crusty and domed, level it with a knife (save these bits for decoration), then cut the cake horizontally into 3 even slices. Lay the base slice onto a cake plate or stand. Spread on about 4-5 tablespoons of the frosting, sandwich the next layer on, and then repeat with another 4-5 tablespoons of frosting and place the final layer on top. Take half the remaining frosting and ice the sides of the cake, leveling it out to be smooth (the layer should be about ⅛in/3mm thick). Pour the remaining frosting on top and level it out flat. I make black crumbs by processing the excess cake in a food processor to sprinkle neatly around the edge of the cake.

SERVES 8-10
....

PREPARATION TIME
20 minutes, plus cooling

COOKING TIME
1¼ hours

COCONUT, BANANA & PINEAPPLE CAKE

This is a totally tropical cake, but (due to its snowball appearance) makes an awesome holiday dessert.

....

Heat the oven to 325°F (170°C) and lightly grease an 8in (20cm) diameter springform cake pan.

Using a blender, blend together the bananas and coconut milk to make a smooth paste and set aside. Using a stand mixer, beat together the oil and sugar (alternatively place them in a large bowl and use an electric hand mixer). Add the eggs, one at a time, beating after each addition. Beat this for a good 5 minutes, or until it's really light, pale, and fluffy. Stir in the vanilla extract and the banana and coconut milk mixture.

Whisk together the flour, baking soda, and salt in another bowl, fold the dry ingredients into the wet ingredients until just combined, then stir in 1 cup (120g) of the shredded coconut. Pour the batter into the prepared pan.

Bake for 1–1¼ hours, or until a metal skewer inserted in the center of the cake comes out clean. Leave to cool in the pan. If you think the cake has a thick crust on the top, lay a warm, damp, wrung-out clean dish towel over the top of the cake while it cools and this will soften it.

To make the frosting, beat the cream cheese with the confectioner's sugar. In a separate bowl, whip together the cream and vanilla until thickened. Now beat the cream cheese into the cream until combined. Leave in the fridge to chill while the cake is cooling.

Remove the cake from the pan. If the top is still a little crusty and domed, level it with a knife, and then cut the cake horizontally into 3 even layers. Lay the base slice onto a cake plate or stand. Spread on half the pineapple jam, and then 4–5 tablespoons of the frosting. Sandwich the next layer on, repeat with the rest of the jam and another 4–5 tablespoons of frosting, and then place the final layer on top. Take half of the remaining frosting and ice the sides of the cake (the layer should be about ⅛in/3mm thick). Pour the remaining frosting on top and level it out flat. Cover the top of the cake with the rest of the toasted coconut and you're good to go...

3 medium overripe bananas, mashed
1 cup (250ml) coconut milk
½ cup (120ml) vegetable oil
generous ½ cup (120g) sugar
2 free-range eggs
1 teaspoon vanilla extract
2¾ cups (350g) self-rising flour
½ teaspoon baking soda
½ teaspoon table salt
1½ cups (170g) sweetened shredded coconut, ½ cup (50g) toasted and set aside for the topping
heaped ¼ cup (100g) Pineapple Jam (see page 219)

For the frosting

14oz (400g) cream cheese
1¾ cups (200g) confectioner's sugar
scant 1 cup (200ml) heavy cream
seeds of 1 vanilla pod or 1 teaspoon vanilla extract or vanilla paste

SERVES 4
....

PREPARATION TIME
15 minutes, plus infusing

COOKING TIME
35-40 minutes

WHITE CHOCOLATE
& CHERRY CLAFOUTIS

I still struggle with how to explain what a clafoutis is. It's a French dessert that's somewhere between a popover and custard, and it's sweet and filled with fruit: yeah, that'll do. This one is gluten-free and very custardy. It needs to be a little undercooked, especially since we're going down the chocolate route here. White chocolate and cherry is as good a combination as fish and chips or mac and cheese. To get the best out of this dish, don't let the cherries cook to gunge or the chocolate cook until it's too firm.

....

Chop the chocolate into chunks. Melt the chocolate either in a double boiler (or a heatproof bowl set over a pot of gently simmering water), or in the microwave. Set aside to cool a little so that it's not boiling hot.

Now you need to make the batter. Mix together the cornstarch, sugar, and eggs. Slowly whisk in the milk until combined, then add the cream, vanilla extract, and a pinch of salt. You should now have a thinish batter. Thoroughly beat in the melted chocolate. Now, in the same way that you would let any other batter rest, place the mixture in the fridge for 15 minutes.

Heat the oven to 375°F (190°C). Butter an 11in (28cm) round ovenproof dish, then sprinkle with sugar. Fill the dish with the cherries and then pour in the batter. Bake for 30–35 minutes, or until well risen and golden on top but still with a gentle wobble in the middle. Leave the clafoutis to cool until warm or room temperature—it will firm up a little as it cools. Scoop it out of the dish and serve.

3½oz (100g) white chocolate
  (I like the stuff with vanilla
  seeds in it)
2 tablespoons cornstarch
2½ tablespoons (20g) superfine
  sugar, plus extra for
  sprinkling
6 large free-range eggs
⅔ cup (150ml) milk
1 cup (250ml) heavy cream
1 tablespoon vanilla extract
pinch of table salt
butter, for greasing
1lb (500g) black cherries,
  pitted

WAFFLES WITH BANANAS FOSTER, PINEAPPLE JAM & CHILI & HONEY BUTTER

This is a recipe of epic proportions. There's a lot to do but it's so worth it. My friend Sami inspired this recipe. He lives in LA and is as food-obsessed as me. He couldn't wait to tell me about a waffle dish with bananas Foster and pineapple jam that he had tried while he was away. Not only did it sound delicious but it so resembled Sami, who is the sunniest, happiest creature I know. You can serve this without the ice cream for an epic brunch, but I prefer it with the ice cream as dessert.

···

First, make the bananas Foster. Melt the butter and sugar in a medium saucepan and then fry the bananas, cut-side down, until golden. (Leave the skin on the bananas while frying; this is to keep the bananas in shape.) Remove the bananas from the pan and set aside, cut-side up. This will encourage a crisper caramel on the face of the bananas. Pour the rum into the pan and quickly whisk, then add the cream and spices and cook until you have a silky pouring sauce. Keep warm.

To make the chili and honey butter melt together the butter, honey, and chili powder in a small saucepan. Keep warm.

Now cook your waffles if you haven't already (see method on page 218) and serve the hot waffles straightaway, one per person, slathered in melted chili and honey butter, together with a spoonful of the Pineapple Jam, 2 halves of a (peeled) banana, a couple of spoonfuls of the rum sauce, and a scoop of vanilla ice cream.

For the bananas Foster

3½ tablespoons (50g) butter
6 tablespoons (80g) light
  muscovado sugar
4 bananas (unpeeled), halved
  lengthways
3 tablespoons (40ml) dark rum
scant 1 cup (200ml) heavy cream
pinch of allspice
a good grating of nutmeg

For the chili & honey butter

5½ tablespoons (80g) butter
1 tablespoon runny honey
½ teaspoon hot chili powder

To serve

4 Vanilla Waffles (see page 218)
4 tablespoons Pineapple Jam
  (see page 219)
4 large scoops vanilla
  ice cream

BAKED ROSÉ APRICOTS
WITH SPELT PANCAKES & PISTACHIOS

I was introduced to spelt by the old boss of Mulberry, Roger Saul, who sold up and went to live in Somerset and set up a spelt farm. Spelt flour tastes like a lighter whole-wheat flour and is BRILLIANT for baking. These spelt pancakes are terrific with roasted apricots that are baked with a splash of wine and served with a syrup. Serve with yogurt if you're being good or mascarpone. if you're feeling decadent.

•••

10 fresh, just ripe apricots,
   (about 1¼lb/550g), halved
   and pitted
scant ½ cup (100ml) rosé wine
¼ cup (50g) sugar
1 vanilla pod
2 bay leaves
1 cinnamon stick

For the spelt pancakes

scant ¾ cup (170ml) milk
1 tablespoon white wine vinegar
   or lemon juice
1 cup (100g) spelt flour
1 teaspoon sugar
¼ teaspoon salt
1 teaspoon baking powder
¾ teaspoon baking soda
1 free-range egg, beaten
1 tablespoon olive oil or
   melted butter, plus extra
   for frying

To serve

3 tablespoons Greek yogurt,
   fat-free Greek yogurt, or
   mascarpone cheese
3 tablespoons chopped
   pistachios

Preheat the oven to 375°F (190°C). Place the apricot halves in an ovenproof dish, pour in the wine, and sprinkle with sugar. Split the vanilla pod in half lengthways, scrape out the seeds, and add both the seeds and the pod to the dish with the apricots. Add the bay leaves and cinnamon stick and mix together. Cover with foil and bake for 20 minutes. Remove the foil, gently mix, then re-cover and put it back in the oven for a further 10 minutes. Remove from the oven and let the apricots steam under the foil for 10 minutes, then remove the foil and leave to cool slightly.

Pour out the liquid from the apricots into a small saucepan or frying pan and reduce the liquid over medium-high heat until syrupy, like a light maple syrup.

To make the spelt pancakes, combine the milk and vinegar or lemon juice in a bowl. Set aside to sit and "sour" while you prepare the other ingredients. In a large bowl, combine the spelt flour, sugar, salt, baking powder, and baking soda. Add the beaten egg and oil or melted butter to the soured milk, stir well to combine, then pour into the bowl with the dry ingredients. Stir gently until just combined: the mixture will be lumpy.

Heat a heavy-based frying pan over medium-high heat. Brush the pan with a little olive oil or butter. Pour a ladleful of the batter into the pan (about ¼ cup/60ml of batter for each pancake—I often use a measuring cup instead of a ladle). Cook until the bottom of the pancake is set and browned and bubbles appear on the top, then flip and cook for another 1-2 minutes. Repeat with remaining batter—it will make exactly 8 pancakes. Serve the pancakes hot with the warm apricots, a dollop of yogurt or mascarpone, the syrup poured over, and topped with chopped pistachios.

MAKES 2 PINTS (1 LITER)

....

PREPARATION TIME
10 minutes, plus infusing
and freezing

COOKING TIME 15 minutes

APRICOT KERNEL &
ALMOND MILK ICE CREAM
WITH BAKED ROSÉ APRICOTS

This dessert is so beautiful and elegant; the almond milk is infused with the scent of apricot kernels and some of the kernels are blended into the ice cream. It was a hard recipe to develop and my friend Alex Fubini at the Ice Cream Union helped me to get the quantities just right. You see, there's not much fat in almond milk, or apricot kernels for that matter, and I wanted to try using unrefined rapadura sugar instead of refined white sugar, all of which affect the balance of the recipe, but we got there in the end. This ice cream is just heavenly when served alongside Baked Rosé Apricots.

....

Place the almond milk, almond oil, and kernels in a saucepan and heat until just starting to steam—do not let the milk boil or it will split. Leave to infuse for 2 hours—the infused mik should have a much more rounded apricot and almond tinge to it.

Using a slotted spoon, remove half of the kernels from the milk and discard. Pour the infused milk and the remaining kernels into a food processor and blend until smooth, and then add the salt. Now, return the mixture to the pan and heat again until it is steaming but not boiling.

In a large bowl, whisk together the egg yolks, sugar, and xanthan gum until fluffy. Whisk in the hot infused milk and kernels mixture and then pour it all back into the pan. There is now enough fat and sugar to stabilize the mixture, so place the pan over low heat and whisk until the mixture comes up to a boil and thickens to a rich custard. Remove from the heat, cover the surface of the custard with a layer of plastic wrap, and set aside to cool.

Once cool, pour the custard into an ice cream machine and churn according to the manufacturer's instructions until it's frozen. Transfer to a 1-quart (1-liter) sealable plastic container and freeze for a minimum of 5 hours. Serve with Baked Rosé Apricots and sprinkled with crushed Amaretti biscuits.

4¼ cups (1 liter) best-quality
  pressed almond milk (I use
  The Pressery brand)
1½ tablespoons sweet almond oil
3½oz (100g) apricot kernels
  (you can now buy these from
  health food stores—yippee!)
½ teaspoon salt
8 free-range egg yolks
⅔ cup (130g) rapadura sugar or
  ½ cup (110g) white sugar
½ teaspoon xanthan gum
Baked Rosé Apricots, to serve
  (see page 200)
Amaretti biscuits, crushed, to
  serve

You will also need an ice cream
  maker

MAKES 10 SLICES
....

PREPARATION TIME
20 minutes, plus chilling and
cooling

COOKING TIME 1½ hours

MAPLE SYRUP, ORANGE & ROSEMARY TART

If you asked me to choose a favorite dessert it'd be hard, but if I HAD TO then one of the best has got to be the British classic, treacle tart. I bloody love it, especially warm from the oven with crème fraîche. I'm a sucker for some rosemary and salt with anything sweet (it just works), so I tried to create a maple syrup version of this tart with orange as the main flavor, infused with some rosemary for good measure. And do you know what? It was a revelation! It beats treacle tart hands down. Don't believe me? Try it!

....

Heat the oven to 375°F (190°C). Dust your countertop with flour and roll out the pastry so it's really thin (about 2mm thick). Very carefully line a deep 9in (23cm) diameter tart pan with the pastry, leaving the excess pastry overhanging the edge of the pan (this will be trimmed off after the pastry has been blind-baked). Place the pastry-lined pan in the freezer for 10 minutes. Line the raw pastry base with parchment paper, fill it with baking beans, and blind-bake for 20 minutes. Remove the baking beans and paper and put it back in the oven for a further 10 minutes. Remove from the oven and leave to cool. Lower the oven temperature to 275°F (140°C). When the pastry base is cool, use a knife to carefully trim the edges, carving off the excess against the side of the pan. Use a pastry brush to brush away any crumbs.

Put the orange and lemon zest and juices in a saucepan with the rosemary, golden syrup, maple syrup, butter, and salt. Bring to a boil and then remove from the heat and leave to cool until the mixture is warm enough to sip. This should now have a really great balance of citrus, rosemary, and maple syrup flavors and will be very sweet. Remove and discard the rosemary sprigs, since we don't want those in the tart, just the flavor of rosemary infused into the dish.

In a bowl, mix together the citrus syrup with the breadcrumbs and leave to stand for 5 minutes so that the breadcrumbs absorb the syrup. Mix in the egg and egg yolk, then spoon the mixture into the pastry base and bake for 50–60 minutes until it is set but still has a bit of a wobble in the center. Remove from the oven and leave to cool for 10 minutes before serving with crème fraîche.

all-purpose flour, for dusting
9oz (250g) ready-made, ready-rolled sweet shortcrust pastry (pâte sucrée if you can find it)
zest and juice of 2 oranges
zest and juice of 1 lemon
4–5 rosemary sprigs
1 cup (350g) golden syrup (from the British food section of a supermarket)
¾ cup (170ml) maple syrup
1 tablespoon (15g) butter
½ teaspoon sea salt flakes
4oz (110g) fresh breadcrumbs
1 free-range egg plus 1 egg yolk, lightly beaten
crème fraîche, to serve

....

SERVES 6 (it's rich)
....

PREPARATION TIME
20 minutes, plus setting

COOKING TIME
25–30 minutes

MOLTEN CARAMEL & CHOCOLATE CAKES

Chocolate with salted caramel is the best dessert combination ever. If it (or rhubarb) is on the menu then I have to order it—and I'm not especially a dessert person. Here is the ultimate version of this combination of ingredients: a baked chocolate dessert with a molten base of salted caramel. It's hot, it's gooey, it's salty, sweet, and chocolaty, and it's messy home cooking. I don't think you've eaten this right unless it's all over your face and you're licking the dish.

....

Butter 6 medium ramekins or individual baking dishes, each about 4¼in (11cm) in diameter and 2in (5cm) deep, then dust with rice flour.

To make the caramel, melt the sugar with a splash of water in a saucepan over medium heat until it is a light golden color. Whisk in the butter, then the cream, and finally the salt. Pour the caramel about ½in (1cm) deep into the base of each prepared ramekin or dish, then leave in the fridge for 20 minutes to set. Reserve any caramel leftover for serving.

When the caramel has almost set, start making the chocolate pudding. Preheat the oven to 275°F (140°C). Melt together the butter, chocolate, cocoa powder, and salt in a double boiler (or a heatproof bowl set over a pot of gently simmering water), stirring until it is smooth. In a separate bowl, beat the eggs and sugar together until light and well creamed. Beat in the maple syrup, vanilla extract, and cream, then pour in the chocolate mixture and mix well. Pour on top of the set caramel and bake in the oven for 25–30 minutes, or until it's puffed up and set on top but still has a slight wobble in the very center. Remove from the oven and leave to sit for 5 minutes. Serve with a dollop of crème fraîche and any leftover caramel.

1 stick plus 2½ tablespoons (150g) unsalted butter, plus extra for greasing
1 tablespoon rice flour, for dusting
5½oz (160g) good-quality chocolate
½ cup (60g) cocoa powder
small pinch of sea salt flakes
4 free-range eggs
1 cup (200g) sugar
3 tablespoons maple syrup
1 teaspoon vanilla extract
3 tablespoons heavy cream
crème fraîche, to serve

For the caramel

¾ cup (150g) sugar
4½ tablespoons (65g) butter, diced
scant ½ cup (100ml) heavy cream
1 teaspoon sea salt flakes

SERVES 4
....

PREPARATION TIME
10 minutes, plus soaking and
standing

COOKING TIME 20 minutes

THAI STICKY RICE WITH MANGO

I'm dedicating another recipe to one of my greatest friends of all time, my "wifey," Zoe Willis. Willis and I went to Thailand together and spent our time eating some incredible food, traveling around, experiencing not a single same thing—except maybe our obsession with sticky rice and mango. It was like our home comfort. When we got home after an epic day, we would get into bed, order some sticky rice, and watch a flick. In a place of insane, sticky rice made us sane. It's our thing. So this one's for you, Zoe...

....

Place the glutinous rice in a bowl, cover with cold water, and leave covered for 1 hour. You can leave it up to 5 hours, but the rice starts to break down a bit.

Okay, so this is where it gets a bit annoying if you're not used to it: steaming the rice. I use a bamboo steamer and I line it with wet cheesecloth or even strong paper towel is fine. Drain and wash the rice, and then tip it into the lined steamer. Cover with some more wet cloth or paper towel and put the lid on the steamer. Place the steamer in a lidded pan of boiling water, where the water only just reaches up to the base of the steamer. I use a lidded wok for this. Put the lid on and steam the rice at a low to medium simmer for 20 minutes. Alternatively, if you own a proper steamer, just steam the rice in the muslin or paper towel for 20 minutes according to the steamer instructions.

Meanwhile, make a coconut caramel. Heat the coconut milk in a small pan over high heat, add the palm sugar and salt, and stir until dissolved. Bring to a boil for a few seconds, then turn off the heat.

When the rice has steamed and cooked all the way through with no crunchy bits in the middle, turn it out into a mixing bowl. Pour on the coconut caramel and give it a good mix. Next, cover the bowl with plastic wrap and leave for 30 minutes. The rice will absorb all the coconut and it will be well seasoned. And completely sticky.

Now here's the hard part; technically, you should wait until it's at room temperature to eat it. Sometimes I can do this, other times not a hope. Serve with sliced mango and sprinkled with sesame seeds.

heaped 1 cup (220g) Thai
glutinous rice (also known as
sticky rice or sweet rice)
¾ cup (170ml) creamy coconut
milk
2oz (60g) palm sugar, grated or
finely chopped
½ teaspoon sea salt flakes
1 really good ripe mango,
peeled, pitted, and sliced
toasted black and white sesame
seeds, to serve

BASICS

PREPARATION TIME
10 minutes

COOKING TIME
3½ hours

WHITE CHICKEN STOCK
& OTHER HOMEMADE STOCK

Stock—making is a slow process but I find it really therapeutic, and I'm a huge advocate because it means you are using every last morsel of an animal. I save chicken carcasses in a bag in the freezer after I've had a roast chicken and, in fact, I also save any other leftover chicken on the bone. If you have trouble finding raw carcasses, then you can use about 1¾lb (800g) of chicken wings instead. Fresh chicken stock is great in brothy or puréed soups, stews, gravies, and wherever else it is called for. It freezes brilliantly, so invest in lots of 1 pint (400ml) sealable plastic containers and then you can have stock on hand whenever you need it. I've included a few other recipes using the same basic method for when you might need other flavored stocks.

3 roast chicken carcasses (after each roast meal remember to put the carcass into a bag and freeze it until you have enough saved up) or 3–4 raw chicken carcasses (these can be bought from your butcher)
1 pig's trotter, cut into slices by a butcher (optional—this makes a really gelatinous stock)
2 onions, quartered
1 bulb of garlic, halved horizontally
2 carrots, chopped into 3 pieces
2 leeks, chopped into 3 pieces
a few fresh herbs, such as parsley stalks and thyme sprigs
1 bay leaf
8 black peppercorns

Place all the ingredients in a large, deep saucepan, cover with cold water, and slowly bring to a boil. Scum will rise to the surface as the stock begins to boil so use a large spoon or a small ladle to skim off the scum and any fat. When the stock has reached boiling point, reduce the heat and gently simmer the stock for 3 hours, skimming the top as it cooks—most of the skimming will need to be done during the first 30 minutes of cooking time. (It's important to make sure the stock doesn't boil at this stage or the bubbles will knock away at the proteins and make the stock cloudy.) As the stock cooks it will begin to reduce; if the water level falls below the contents of the pot, add a little more cold water—this will reveal any scum hiding at the bottom of the pan.

When the 3 hours are up, place a fine sieve over a large pan or bowl and strain the stock to collect all the flavorsome juices. At this stage, the stock may not have much flavor so you will need to slowly reduce the liquid in order for the flavors to be condensed. To do this, pour the stock into a pan, bring the stock to a boil, reduce the heat, and simmer to slowly reduce the stock, tasting it every so often, until you have the right intensity of chickenyness. Do not season your stock. Obviously, the stock will taste better if you season it but it will still need tweaking once it's used in other dishes so it's better to leave it unseasoned for now.

You can use the stock straightaway or let it cool and then transfer it to the fridge or freezer. A good chicken stock will have a really chickeny essence and it will turn to jelly when it is refrigerated.

Dark chicken stock: For a richer stock that's great with gravies and meat stews, roast the veggies and chicken carcasses in a really hot oven for 30 minutes, or until they have become golden and caramelized (be careful not to burn them or the charred flavor will transfer to the stock), then cook the stock as opposite.

Beef or veal stock: Swap the chicken carcasses for 4½lb (2kg) of beef or veal shin bones and cook in the same way as for the dark chicken stock, cooking the stock for 3–4 hours before straining. Veal stock is the best to use when making meat gravies, since it will give you that flavor you normally only get in restaurants.

Fish stock: Swap the chicken carcasses for the carcasses (but not heads) of 3 largish white fish or 2¼lb (1kg) of fish bones. Salmon or tuna make horrible stock so I would go for sea bass, halibut, haddock, and so on. Cook in the same way as for the white chicken stock, but only cook the stock for 20 minutes before straining. There is a fine line when it comes to making fish stock and it can become quite rancid if cooked for too long.

Veggie stock: Leave out the chicken carcasses and double the quantity of vegetables in the white chicken stock recipe, adding 2 parsnips and some of the outer leaves of a cabbage. Place in a large saucepan, cover with cold water, and cook gently for 20 minutes. As with fish stock, vegetable stock can taste and smell too strong if it's cooked for too long—think of the stewed veggies you used to get at school!

PREPARATION TIME
5 minutes

COOKING TIME
10 minutes

CAULIFLOWER RICE

Everyone is going nuts for spiralized vegetables and vegetable rices. I wasn't convinced about them to begin with but the whole "don't knock it 'til you try it" rule absolutely came into its own here. My friend Elly, who owns Pear Café in Bristol, whips up some of the most incredible low-calorie concoctions that are a 5:2 dieter's dream. It was at a pop-up that Elly organized where I first tried cauliflower rice, in a salad with purple cauliflower, tahini, and Sriracha chili sauce. It was delicious. The cauliflower had lost its strong flavor and was a terrific medium for soaking up sauce! The recipe is so simple, I'm now hooked and into trying out loads of rice and couscous recipes with this method. Serve it with Pulled Chipotle Chicken (see page 175) or Dhal with Spiced Heirloom Carrots, Tofu & Cashews (see page 186).

Place the cauliflower in a food processor and pulse it until it resembles something the size of rice.

Heat the oil or butter in a frying pan with a lid. Throw in the cauliflower and cook over high heat for a minute or so to sear the outside, stirring continuously. You don't want the cauliflower to color, so keep it moving.

Pour in the stock, add some salt, and cover with the lid. Cook for 5 minutes, then remove the lid and cook until the stock has reduced into the rice. It's now ready to serve.

1 cauliflower, about 9–11oz
  (250–300g), trimmed
1 tablespoon oil or butter of
  your choice
3½ tablespoons (50ml) fresh
  White Chicken, Fish, or Beef
  Stock (see pages 212–13, or
  water is fine)
a good pinch of sea salt flakes

PREPARATION TIME
5 minutes

COOKING TIME
10 minutes

HOLLANDAISE SAUCE

Don't freak out at the idea of making hollandaise sauce. There are foodie scaremongers out there but it's really not that tricky to make this sauce, all you need is patience. Just let the butter trickle really, really slowly into the food processor and watch your sauce turn from slick butter into a thick, emulsified sauce. It doesn't keep very well, so it's best to make it to order. For béarnaise sauce, which is an absolute classic with steak, just add chopped tarragon and chervil to your finished hollandaise.

To make the reduction, place all the ingredients in a small saucepan and bring to a boil. Keep boiling to reduce the amount of liquid until you have just 2 tablespoons left. Strain the reduction into a cold bowl.

Whizz the egg yolks in a food processor with a pinch of salt and then pour in half the reduction.

With the machine running, pour the butter into the food processor very, very slowly—1 teaspoon at a time—until half of it has been used up (the sauce should be fairly thick at this point). Pour in the remaining butter in a fine stream until it has all combined. Season the sauce with salt, lemon juice, and the remaining reduction if it needs it.

Alternatively, you can make the sauce by hand, beating the ingredients together with a balloon whisk or an electric hand mixer in a double boiler (or a heatproof bowl set over a bowl of gently simmering water).

For the reduction

1 shallot, finely chopped
6 tablespoons white wine
  vinegar
3 black peppercorns
1 bay leaf
2 blades of mace

For the sauce

4 free-range egg yolks
sea salt flakes
2 sticks (225g) hot melted
  butter
squeeze of lemon juice

SCHMALTZ & GRIBENES

PREPARATION TIME
10 minutes
COOKING TIME 40 minutes

Most people know very little about Jewish food. Many of us will have heard of, or possibly even tried, chopped liver (it's a coarse pâté) but not many people who aren't Jewish or "au fait" with Jewish cuisine will be familiar with gribenes. They are a by-product of making schmaltz (chicken fat that is rendered down and then used to cook and flavor dishes). What you're left with after making schmaltz is little nuggets of chicken skin. These are then rendered down even more but this time with onions, until you have crisp roasted chicken skin with caramelized onions. Gribenes are the stuff that dreams are made of, and they're used to garnish numerous dishes. I use them in Chopped Liver with Egg & Gribenes (see page 65) and in the Egg & Onions sandwich (see page 89).

With scissors or a sharp knife, cut the chicken skin into ¼–½in (8–10mm) cubes.

Heat a frying pan over medium-low heat and add the chicken skin. Increase the heat until the skin starts to fry, then reduce the temperature until it is fairly low and cook the chicken skin very slowly for 25–30 minutes, or until the fat has rendered out of it. The chicken skin should let out about 1¼ cups (300ml) of fat. You need to fry the skin slowly over low heat, since you don't want any color to the skin. Strain the fat from the chicken skin, reserving the fat (schmaltz) since it is as precious as gold dust.

Return the chicken skin to the pan. There is no need to wipe out the pan—you will need the excess chicken fat to help the skin crisp up. Fry the skin for 2 minutes, or until some more fat starts to come out. Then add the onion and sauté with the chicken skin until the onions break down and start to caramelize. Season with salt and continue to fry until the skin is roasted and has turned golden and the onions have caramelized. Pour any excess fat into the reserved schmaltz and drain the gribenes on paper towel, adding more salt if necessary, and allow to crisp up.

The schmaltz will last up to a month in the fridge but I suggest you use the gribenes on the day you make them.

1lb (500g) raw chicken skin (you can buy this from a butcher or collect it whenever you skin some chicken and freeze until you have enough for this recipe)
½ onion, very thinly sliced
a good pinch of sea salt flakes

PREPARATION TIME
30 minutes

FERMENTING TIME
24 hours–2 weeks

GIZZI'S KIMCHI

MY LIFE REVOLVES around kimchi. It's my lifeline. I love it so much I even called my cat Kimchi. The hot, tangy, crunchy, cabbage is in my veins! It's an acquired taste and takes a bit of time to get your head around it. If I'm honest, I actually prefer it served in a Western way, rather than a Korean way, such as in grilled cheese or with cured meats. Anyway, for those who are new to it, it's a fermented cabbage, a bit like sauerkraut, but oh so very fiery! You make it a couple of weeks in advance, a bit like pickles or chutney, and allow it to naturally ferment and go sour. It's served in Korea as an accompaniment to almost every dish. There are at least two recipes in this book that use it, so it's good to have a supply you've made yourself (although I do sometimes buy store-bought stuff from the Asian supermarkets). It's fun to make and it's messy. Try it at least once. The longer it ferments, the tangier it gets. I like mine really tangy and fizzy, but most people like it quite light.

1 small to medium head of Chinese Napa cabbage

⅓ cup plus 1 tablespoon (50g) sea salt flakes (I use Maldon)

¼ cup (50g) plus 2 tablespoons sugar

1 bulb of garlic, cloves separated

3oz (80g) peeled fresh ginger root

½ cup (50–60g) kochukaru (or gochugaru, Korean chili powder)

2¾ tablespoons (40ml) fish sauce

2¾ tablespoons (40ml) usukuchi (light Korean soy sauce)

1 tablespoon jarred salted shrimp

6 scallions (green and white parts), julienned

1 Korean pear or sharp apple, such as Granny Smith, peeled, cored, and julienned

Trim the outside leaves off of the cabbage, and then cut the cabbage into quarters through the root.

In a saucepan, heat about 1¼ cups (300ml) water, add the salt and ¼ cup (50g) sugar, and stir until dissolved. Pour into a really large non-reactive container that will hold the cabbage and cover with 17 cups (4 liters) of cold water. If the water is totally cool, add the cabbage and leave to brine overnight.

Blend the garlic, ginger, kochukaru, fish sauce, usukuchi, shrimp, and remaining sugar in a food processor until completely puréed. If it is very thick and sludgey, add water about ¼ cup (60ml) at a time until it becomes a custard-like consistency. Stir in the scallions and pear or apple.

Drain the cabbage and rub the marinade into every leaf. Wedge the quarters into a 3-quart (3-liter) Kilner jar or the largest jar you can find, then refrigerate. The kimchi will be tasty after 24 hours, but it will be better in a week and at its prime in 2 weeks. It will still be good for another couple weeks after that, though it will grow way stronger and funkier.

VANILLA WAFFLES

This is a really simple recipe to ensure really light, fluffy waffles that have hints of vanilla. Serve them the American way, with smoked streaky bacon and real maple syrup; the Belgian way, slathered in chocolate sauce; or my way (see page 197), with chili and honey butter, pineapple jam, and bananas Foster.

·······································

Preheat a waffle iron according to the manufacturer's instructions.

Sift together the flour, baking powder, salt, and sugar in a bowl. In a separate bowl, whisk together the milk, egg yolks, and vanilla extract and pour it over the dry ingredients, stirring very gently until half combined. Pour in the melted butter and continue mixing until the batter is fully combined.

In a separate, spotlessly clean bowl, whisk the egg whites until stiff, and then fold them into the batter until fully combined and you have a smooth, fluffy batter.

Brush the waffle iron with a little melted butter and then pour a ladleful of the batter into the iron and cook for 6–8 minutes, or until the waffle is crisp and golden. Repeat with the rest of the mixture and set aside the cooked waffles under a clean dish towel to keep warm. Serve the waffles piping hot with whichever toppings you like.

Store any leftover batter in the fridge for up to 2 days.

generous ¾ cup (250g)
  all-purpose flour
2 teaspoons baking powder
½ teaspoon salt
¼ cup (50g) sugar
1 cup (250ml) milk
2 free-range egg yolks
1 tablespoon vanilla extract
1 stick (110g) unsalted butter,
  melted, plus extra for
  brushing
4 free-range egg whites

You will also need a waffle iron

·······································

PREPARATION TIME
10 minutes

COOKING TIME
55 minutes

PINEAPPLE JAM

Everyone said that you couldn't make pineapple jam. Everyone lied. You can—and it's amazing. You just need to give it a bit of a pectin-boost. I use jam sugar, which has pectin already added (look for this online). But if you would rather use regular sugar, buy a low- or no-sugar pectin and follow the package instructions for how much to add and at what stage (this varies depending on the brand). Don't do what I always do, which is to try and eat scalding sugar off a metal spoon immediately after its cooked: that's just stupid...

Cut the pineapple into large chunks. Put them in a food processor and pulse until the pineapple has broken down into ¼in (5mm) pieces. It is best to use a food processor, since the pineapple releases a lot of juice, but if you don't have one then hand-chopping finely with a cross-chop motion is okay.

Place the pineapple in a medium saucepan, cover with a scant 1 cup (200ml) water, and cook slowly for 3 minutes, or until the pineapple is soft. (If you are using regular sugar, measure the pulp at this point and consult your pectin package for how much to add and when.)

Add the sugar and lime or lemon juice and stir over low heat until the sugar grains have melted. Cook for another 45 minutes, or until the pineapple has become like a loose jam. It will thicken a bit on cooling, so you only need about 2 tablespoons of liquid left in the base of the pan.

Pour the jam into a sterilized jar, top with a piece of wax paper, allow to cool fully, and seal tightly. You can store this in the fridge for up to 3 months. I would leave the jam to mature and develop its flavor for at least a week before eating, though it's obviously fine to eat it straightaway once cool.

1 large pineapple, skinned and cored (to make about 1¼lb/ 550g flesh)
1¼ cups (250g) jam sugar (or use regular sugar and 1 package low- or no-sugar pectin)
3½ tablespoons (50ml) lime or lemon juice

INDEX

INDEX